T0065401

DEALING WITH MEMORY CHANGES AS YOU GROW OLDER

DEALING WITH MEMORY CHANGES AS YOU GROW OLDER

**Kathleen Gose, M.S.W.,
and Gloria Levi, M.S.**

BANTAM BOOKS
NEW YORK · TORONTO · LONDON · SYDNEY · AUCKLAND

DEALING WITH MEMORY CHANGES AS YOU GROW OLDER
*A Bantam Book / published by arrangement with
the authors*

Library of Congress Cataloging-in-Publication Data

Gose, Kathleen.
Dealing with memory changes as you grow older.

Reprint. Originally published: Toronto : McClelland-
Bantam, c1985. (Seal books)
Bibliography: p.
1. Memory in old age. I. Levi, Gloria. II. Title.
BF724.85.M45G68   1988   155.67   88-47682
ISBN 978-0-553-34597-1 (pbk.)

Published simultaneously in the United States and Canada

*Bantam Books are published by Bantam Books, a division of
Bantam Doubleday Dell Publishing Group, Inc. Its trademark,
consisting of the words "Bantam Books" and the portrayal of
a rooster, is Registered in U.S. Patent and Trademark Office
and in other countries. Marca Registrada. Bantam Books,
666 Fifth Avenue, New York, New York 10103.*

PM691 0654

CONTENTS

PART II. Dealing With Memory Changes

INTRODUCTION

HOW THIS HANDBOOK CAME ABOUT

Both authors of this book have worked with older adults for many years; Kathy with people in the community, Gloria with people both in the community and in care facilities. We have been struck many times by the concerns and anxieties voiced by seniors about their changing abilities to remember.

This led us to explore what has been written about memory and aging, what has been written specifically for older adults on the subject, and what is being done about memory training courses for older people. We discovered that there is a growing amount of research on memory and aging, quite a bit of it still in the "wait and see" stage. But there is very little written directly for older adults and there are few classes dealing with their memory changes.

In 1978 we conducted a ten-hour program in memory training at the Summer Session for Seniors at the University of British Columbia. The response was quite startling. Many more people than we could accommodate wanted to enroll in the program. Some of the people on the waiting list were very insistent about their need for such a course.

Since that time we have offered many courses separately and jointly, revising and reworking material to meet the needs of the people we have taught. As time passed, we began to consider writing a book specifically for older people on normal memory changes. We reviewed the literature, spoke to other professionals, and discussed our ideas with older people. We also did a considerable amount of soul searching about the relevance to older adults of much that is offered as memory training. From all this emerged *Dealing With Memory Changes as You Grow Older.*

WHO THIS BOOK IS FOR

This book is written for adults who are in reasonable health and living independently. It is not intended for people who are suffering from serious brain disorders, or are severely handicapped, clinically depressed, or on heavy dosage of medications which affect the central nervous system. The book is for people who are experiencing the normal memory changes of aging and are interested in learning more about them and how to handle them effectively.

WHAT THE HANDBOOK IS ABOUT

We have come to realize that a book written specifically for older adults must contain much more than the techniques to a better memory which are offered in memory training books aimed at the general public. While some information in these books is useful, much of it is not relevant to older people.

Our book has taken a broad, inclusive approach to the subject of normal memory changes because there are many physical and psychological influences which play a part in those changes. The purpose of the book is threefold: 1) to give the reader an understanding of the basic principles of how the memory works; 2) to offer the reader a range of memory aids which can be useful in certain circumstances; 3) to explore the issues of remembering as they relate to aging and to personal lifestyle.

This is a handbook, defined by the dictionary as "a small guidebook, reference book, or book of instructions." We have organized it for easy reference and hope that it will serve as a guide to the reader. We have also included a number of quizzes, exercises and examples relevant to our readers to help explain various points and ideas. We invite the reader to get involved with the material rather than simply to read through the book.

We have been assisted by a group of advisors, older men and women who have helped us in early revisions of the manuscript. We have also received help from members of classes in two senior centers. They supplied many ideas for the chapter on practical strategies for remembering, and told us a lot about how they feel and what they do when they have problems with forgetting. One of the pleasures of writing this book has been working with the people who contributed directly to some of its pages from their own experiences with remembering and forgetting.

A word about the use of "he." Most readers of this book were no doubt trained, as we were, to use the pronoun "he" to represent both men and women in general (as in "To each his own"). We agree that it is important to recognize women as women, and we also recognize that there are many more older women than men. The more precise and egalitarian use of pronouns would be she/he or he/she. But in our opinion this is clumsy to write and quickly becomes tedious to read. Therefore, for ease of style we have usually used "he" and sometimes "she" to stand for men and women in general. We have also used various ways to include both sexes at once in our sentences.

MANY THANKS

This book could not have been published without the financial assistance of the Health Promotion Directorate of Health and Welfare Canada. We are very grateful for this support. The ideas in the book are the authors', or come from our research, and do not necessarily reflect the official policy of Health and Welfare Canada.

We also wish to thank the Council of Senior Citizens Organizations (COSCO) which as our official sponsor administered the contribution of the Health Promotion Directorate and gave us their encouragement and support. Some of their members served on our advisory committee and followed our progress with interest.

We appreciate the important contribution made to this book by our senior advisors who patiently read through the manuscript, pointing out problems and making suggestions for improvements. Members of this group are Charles Bayley, Clifford Fenner, Evelyn Olson, Mary Rupp, Marjorie Smith and Arthur Sweet. We are also grateful to our professional colleagues for their advice and support.

Our thanks to Margo Palmer of the Health Promotion Directorate, whose encouragement and keen editorial eye have helped us along the way. We also thank Elliott Gose for several contributions to the book, both general and personal, for clear-headed readings of the manuscript, and helpful suggestions for revision.

Working jointly on a book such as this has had its highs and lows. We thank our families and friends, who have heard about both, sometimes in great detail, and who have always supported and encouraged us.

PART I

Understanding How Memory Works

CHAPTER I

You and Your Memory

HOW MEMORY SERVES US

"I've a grand memory for forgetting," said Alan Breck in *Kidnapped*. As we grow older many of us know what Robert Louis Stevenson's character means. Our own memories seem good at forgetting.

Although we may be concerned about changes in our ability to remember, our memories are still remarkable. Throughout our lives memory plays a major part in defining who we are. Memory serves us in many ways.

- It is the basis of all knowledge we have about ourselves and the world.
- It registers, stores, and makes available information about countless things we have experienced in life, from childhood to a moment ago.
- It records our emotions and feelings.
- It is used in the performance of all the skills we have, from riding a bicycle, knitting, driving a car, to speaking our own, or a foreign language.

1

- It records our sensory experiences and makes it possible to recognize something we have seen before, or can see in the mind's eye; something we have heard before, or can hear in our minds; or to recognize an odor, a taste, a touch.

Everything we know is in our memories.

Our memories have the capacity to store more than any computer yet invented.

Our ability to remember makes each of us a unique person.

It is easy not to notice all that we remember—to take all this for granted. We tend to dwell on what we forget; but the fact is, we have trouble remembering only certain things from our vast stores of memory.

Still it is irritating and sometimes disheartening to find that you have forgotten a name or a fact that you heard only yesterday. Many older people notice that their memory plays more tricks on them than it did when they were younger. This can sometimes be upsetting and worrisome. It is not possible to strengthen your memory the way you might strengthen your muscles, but it is possible to make it work more efficiently.

WHAT THIS HANDBOOK IS ABOUT

If you are looking for ways to improve your memory, this handbook can help you.
The handbook includes:

1. Information about how memory works.
2. Information about how aging affects memory.

3. Practical suggestions for remembering which are used by older people.
4. Instructions about how to use certain memory aids.
5. Information on the impact of health and lifestyle on memory.

To help you understand how memory works the handbook explains the Three R's, REGISTERING, RETAINING, and RETRIEVING. The book also looks at some of the reasons why people forget.

You will find practical suggestions by older people that may help you cope with everyday forgetting. They may also make you aware of how well you are already managing.

Memory aids, or mnemonic techniques, which can be used in certain circumstances, are also introduced.

The book gives a perspective on the changes in memory which come with increasing age. It considers the effects of energy levels and stress on memory, and discusses intelligence and learning during later life. The subject of senility and related disorders is also explored.

The book deals with the relationship between lifestyle and memory. The way you live—eating, resting, moving about, playing and working—all affect memory. The handbook emphasizes the interconnectedness of body, mind, and spirit. Finally the book explores the significant role of memory in the development of the whole human being and in the gaining of wisdom.

A narrow approach to improving your memory by learning a few memory aids may prove disappointing to anyone interested in the effects of aging and memory. A broad understanding of how your mind, body, and spirit work together provides a firm basis for

---

THINGS EASILY REMEMBERED

✔ Names of favorite family members

✔ An important and desirable appointment

✔ Reading and writing skills

✔ Stories, verses or songs from the past

✔ Your birthdate

✔ Paying the rent or mortgage payment

✔ Some of the contents of an interesting lecture, article or favorite TV show

✔ Physical skills such as riding a bicycle or knitting

✔ Routine and habit

---

making long-lasting gains in dealing with memory changes. This book can act as a guide. Choose what works for you.

Pinpointing Your Difficulties in Forgetting

You may have selected this book because you are concerned about your memory changes. In everyday matters you may be experiencing some forgetting. Do

THINGS EASILY FORGOTTEN

- ☑ Where things are
- ☑ Changed routine
- ☑ Things you believe you cannot remember
- ☑ Things you don't want to do
- ☑ Names
- ☑ Trivial information
- ☑ Things forgotten under stress, fatigue, feeling low or sick
- ☑ Boring information
- ☑ Dates

you forget specific things or things in general? Some things are easily remembered and some easily forgotten.

It might be helpful to pinpoint your forgetting difficulties. The following questionnaire asks about everyday memory slips. It asks you to look at how often you forget certain things, what your feelings are when you forget, and what you do when you forget.

QUESTIONNAIRE ON FORGETTING

Rate yourself on these common memory problems:
1. Put a check in the appropriate box, indicating how often this kind of forgetting happens to you.
2. Comment on how this makes you feel.
3. Comment on what you do when this happens.

You forget the name of:	never	seldom	sometimes	often	usually	How does this make you feel?	What do you do when it happens?
1. a person you have recently met.							
2. an old friend you have met by chance.							
3. a friend you are introducing.							
4. a book you are recommending to a friend.							

You have forgotten to do certain things:	never	seldom	sometimes	often	usually	How does this make you feel?	What do you do when it happens?
1. to take your medication, or wonder if you have taken it.							
2. to buy something on your shopping list.							
3. to bring your umbrella, or something else.							
4. to defrost food for dinner.							
5. to keep an appointment.							

7

You have forgotten:	never	seldom	sometimes	often	usually	How does this make you feel?	What do you do when it happens?
6. to do something you promised to do.							
7. to pay your phone or electric bill.							
8. to turn the car headlights off, or the iron.							

You have forgotten:						How does this make you feel?	What do you do when it happens?
1. where you left your glasses, keys.							
2. what you were going to say.							

You have forgotten:	never	seldom	sometimes	often	usually	How does this make you feel?	What do you do when it happens?
3. how much sugar you put in your coffee or tea.							
4. if you have already told somebody something.							
5. what it was you came for.							
6. the details of a story you are telling.							

You forget some things you have read, heard, or seen:	never	seldom	sometimes	often	usually	How does this make you feel?	What do you do when it happens?
1. details of something you have recently read, or heard, or seen on TV, etc.							
2. you start to read something, then remember you have read it before.							
3. other things you tend to forget: a.							
b.							
c.							

1. What kinds of things do you forget more than others?
   Names?
   Things you intend to do?
   Where things are?
   Things that have happened?
2. Were you surprised by the things you usually remember? Usually forget?
3. How do your feelings play a part in how well you function when you forget?
4. Are you satisfied with what you do when you forget?

Your answers to the questionnaire on forgetting tell you something about how well your memory works in everyday situations, how you feel about forgetting in these situations, and what you do when you forget certain things.

Feelings and Forgetting

A REALISTIC LOOK
AT UNPLEASANT FEELINGS

It is easy to be concerned if you find yourself becoming more forgetful. And it is easy to contrast present forgetfulness with your past abilities to remember. Forgetfulness causes unpleasant feelings which can range from embarrassment and frustration to anxiety, humiliation, loss of self-confidence and sometimes even fear. People who are forgetful may begin to feel that they are losing control and start to pay more attention to the times when they can't remember than they do to the times when they can. They begin to wonder if perhaps their forgetfulness is a sign of senility. There can be a snowball effect as stress caused by worry over forgetfulness begins to play a part in their inefficient memories.

Of course, not all older people feel this upset about changes in their memories. When a group of active seniors from a west coast seniors' center answered the questionnaire on forgetting they did not hesitate to reply with many negative descriptions about their feelings, such as: "annoyed," "furious," "cross with myself," "embarrassed," "stupid," "incompetent," "resentment over failing memory," "unsure." In one instance they even felt "ashamed," "guilty," "terrible," and "horrible."

"I'm concerned but not mortified."

However, when these seniors were asked about their negative feelings most of them replied that there is a big difference between how they feel when they forget things and how they feel about themselves as a whole. Although they frequently forget and often get upset over forgetting, they usually don't allow memory problems to get them down for long. Their replies show a matter-of-fact realism:

—"I'm learning to accept my memory. Others are in the same boat."
—"The locks to the filing cabinet grow rusty and slow the process of thinking . . . a lighter attitude towards shortcomings helps."
—"I try not to worry too much but don't rely on my memory as much as I used to. Now I write things down."

—"I try to concentrate and not attempt to do too much at once."

—"I don't lie awake about it."

—"Sometimes I cuss."

—"I'm concerned but not mortified."

There is a big difference between how they feel when they forget things and how they feel about themselves as a whole.

ATTITUDE IS EVERYTHING

How older people handle forgetting usually depends on how they feel about themselves. Many people acknowledge that they have problems remembering, but most of them do not allow forgetfulness to eat away at their self-confidence. They are adjusting, coming to terms with changes that come to aging bodies and minds. They may not like these changes but they find many successful ways of living with them.

One senior has this to say: "In the past couple of years of coping with my increasing physical problems, my memory plays strange games with me, leading to embarrassment, frustration and hilarious situations. For example, I'm taking pool therapy three times a week and carry a tall can of favorite bath powder to facilitate dressing after treatment. Great idea—except the day I reached in to get the bath powder and discovered I had brought the can of hair spray! If I couldn't laugh at myself for these crazy things and memory lapses I'd be in a bad way indeed."

13

Registering, Retaining, Retrieving

THE THREE STAGES IN REMEMBERING

"My memory is not so good anymore."

People often speak of having a "good" or "poor" memory as if it were a tangible part of themselves like a limb or one of the body's organs. Comments such as "He has an excellent memory," or "My memory is not so good anymore," suggest that memory is some thing that either works or doesn't. In reality, most people have good memories for some things and not for others. When they have trouble remembering, it is not because the whole memory is at fault but because part of the memory process is not working efficiently. When people remember, they go through a process of registering new information, retaining or storing it in their brains, and later retrieving it.

Take a simple example from everyday life such as remembering where you put your glasses. First you must become aware of where you place them when you take them off (perhaps next to the lamp on the living room table). You *register* or take notice of what you are doing by paying attention to the action of putting your glasses down at a specific location. This information is stored, or *retained*, ready to be *retrieved*, or brought back.

If all this works, you can *recall* just where you put your glasses. They are where you left them on the table beside the lamp.

This simple example shows the three stages in remembering.

A BREAKDOWN IN THE 3 R'S

There are irritating moments when the three stages don't hold together. You can't remember something because there has been a breakdown somewhere in the process of registering, retaining and retrieving. For example, it is frustrating and demoralizing to turn your whole house upside down looking for something important, such as your Social Security or pension check.

This is what could happen: you sit down quietly and calmly, trying to remember just what you did with the check after you took it out of the mail box. You search each of the most likely places you might have put it. When you can't find it you begin to frown, tense your body and speed up the search. You may feel your heart beating faster—you may get hot and begin to feel more and more flustered. After a while you cannot think clearly. You may even start to panic. It is moments like these, when you are experiencing the stress of forgetting, that may cause you concern about your memory.

When you forget, three things could be happening:

1. You may not have registered clearly to begin with.
2. You may not retain what you have registered.
3. Your retrieval could be faulty.

Difficulties in any one part of the memory process will cause forgetting. Research indicates that older people experiencing memory problems have difficulties with all three parts of the memory system, but especially with registering and retrieving.

When someone asks, "How can I improve my memory?" he is asking the wrong question, according to psychologist Michael J. H. Howe. Howe comments that "the word memory covers a lot of processes, so that to expect to find a simple way of improving memory is about as realistic as to expect to discover a simple way of improving the postal service or the world's economy. It is more realistic to think about how to improve the operation of each of the various [stages] that are necessary for remembering."[1] The stages are registering, retaining and retrieving.

The following chapters on Registering, Retaining and Retrieving explain the Three R's in some detail. They include examples, exercises and quizzes, and will be of interest to those who wish to take a fairly complete look at how the memory works.

For those who want a brief overview, there are summaries at the end of each chapter.

✤

The following books are useful for people who are interested in exploring the subject of memory further:

Higbee, Kenneth L. *Your Memory, How It Works and How to Improve It.* Englewood Cliffs, N.J.; Prentice-Hall, 1977.

Loftus, Elizabeth. *Memory.* Reading, Mass.; Addison-Wesley Publishing Co., 1980.

Minninger, Joan. *Total Recall—How to Boost Your Memory.* Emmaus, Pa.; Rodale Press, 1984.

CHAPTER II

Take Note!—
Registering

Common sense says that registering information is the first step in remembering. If you are going to remember something it has to make some kind of initial impression on you. You obviously cannot recall something which you have never really noticed. The memory operates only when it registers information, events, and experiences which it then records.

Registering

Attitude **Interest** **Attention** **Organization**

ATTITUDE

Attitude is involved in all acts of registering. Whether you are trying to learn something new or to recall

17

something already stored in your memory, your desire to remember it will affect your success. When you intend to remember something, you direct all your attention to it.

Self-confidence also plays an important part in the registering process. Your belief in your ability to remember is essential to remembering.

You may have noticed how hard it is to learn something if you are convinced that it is too difficult. When your grandchild tries to explain what he is doing with his computer you may tend to shut down. When you are introduced to someone with a very different and foreign sounding name you may be convinced that you'll never get it right. The attitude "I *can* learn and I *can* remember" is essential before you can begin to register and record information effectively.

INTEREST

The desire to remember comes from interests, concerns, priorities. People of all ages, but older adults in particular, sort out what they wish to remember, discarding what they don't want to bother with. This sorting out process is usually deliberate and controlled, though at times it is automatic, and done without being noticed.

You may feel that learning about your grandchild's computer is over your head. How it works is neither important nor relevant to you, so why bother? On the other hand, you may be interested in the impact of computers on your local library's catalogue system, so you may feel that this kind of information is worth noting and remembering. Everyone is constantly making decisions about the importance of things and what is worth paying attention to.

DIFFERENT REASONS FOR REMEMBERING

The following five situations suggest different reasons for remembering someone's name. If you were faced with these situations which of the names do you think you might remember? Rank them in order of importance to you, #1 being most important, #5 being least important.

1. The name of someone who owes you $50.
2. The name of someone who works with your neighbor.
3. The name of someone to whom you owe $1.50.
4. The name of someone who brought regards from your nephew.
5. The name of someone who borrowed a book from you.

Interest plays a big role in registering because it sets the stage for paying attention. Your interest in the name of a person who owes you $50 or who borrowed your book may be quite different from your interest in someone who works with your neighbor, or even the name of someone to whom you owe $1.50! You will make an effort to remember what you consider important. Without necessarily being aware of it, you have said to yourself, "I'm going to remember this," or "I'm not going to remember that."

ATTENTION—USING YOUR SENSES

"Attention—perhaps the most wonderful of all
the wondrous powers of the mind."
                    CHARLES DARWIN

Registering depends on paying attention—concentrating and directing your senses to record new information.

Most people's visual sense is their primary one. Bruno Furst, author of *Stop Forgetting*, a popular book on memory training, calls these people "eye-minded." He states that "the eye-minded person benefits most by learning from books or from anything presented visually." However, in some people the sense of hearing is dominant. The "ear-minded" person responds to "the spoken word in general, and anything else produced by sound. . . ."[2] "I see what you mean" or "I see the point" are typical expressions of eye-minded people. Ear-minded people often say "I hear what you are saying" or "I hear your message loud and clear."

Although eye- and ear-mindedness are tremendously important, they are by no means the only senses at work during registering. They are assisted by taste, smell, and touch. These enrich the ability of the visual and auditory senses and at times work on their own during registering. Advice from another memory expert emphasizes this point: "The more senses you bring into play and the more you use the senses that are most effective for you, the better you will remember."[3]

When you pay attention, you focus your mind on certain things and exclude other things. Using several senses helps to focus more fully and to direct your attention. An avid rose gardener visiting a botanical garden is much more likely to remember the display of roses in bloom than he is the other plants. He will pay attention to the variety of colors and shapes, the perfume and the feel of the petals. He may focus his attention on one variety that especially appeals to him. The roses will stand out in his memory, and one particular bush may well outshine all the rest.

On the other hand, people do and see countless things every day to which they do not pay attention. If a woman does not like caviar, she does not focus on the price. But she may pay attention to the price of chicken if she eats it frequently. She may not remember much of what she hears on the radio or TV news unless she listens carefully. It is not that she has "forgotten" the price of caviar or what's on the news, but that she has not registered the information in the first place.

These examples give some idea of the relationship between attitude, interest and attention.

ORGANIZING

One memory researcher comments that a person "who is observing the information that he knows he must later recall . . . is actively processing the material into some form that will later help him to reproduce [it]."[4]

During registering, your brain automatically begins to organize new information. When you register a new experience it does not enter your memory in full, complete detail, as though it were a photograph or a tape recording. Instead, certain impressions or details

21

stick out as highlights and you use them as *clues* to represent the rest of the information entering your memory. Clues summarize more complete and complicated information. Everyone has his or her own personal way of registering information because each person forms his or her own particular clues.

As you register you begin to associate new information with what you already know. The more you can link new clues to information with which you are familiar, the easier it is for you to register the new information.

CHECKING YOUR REGISTERING PROCESS

Attitude, interest, attention and organizing are all involved in the registering process. As you read through statements 1–7 below, assess your strong areas and those which need attention. You might be blaming your memory for its inability to recall when actually your problem could be the result of any of the following difficulties:

	seldom	sometimes	often
1. You lack self-confidence and believe you cannot remember.			
2. You are bored and have no intention of paying attention to information you consider trivial.			
3. You are distracted and do not pay attention.			

	seldom	sometimes	often
4. Your hearing or vision is somewhat impaired and you don't register accurately.			
5. You get flustered and cannot concentrate.			
6. You have difficulty making effective clues that summarize new information.			
7. You have difficulty linking new information with what you already know.			

If you are having trouble registering information, you may find that the chapters in Part II, Common Practical Strategies for Remembering, Other Strategies for Remembering, and Lifestyle and Memory, will be of help.

Registering—Summary

REGISTERING IS THE FIRST STEP IN THE MEMORY PROCESS

REGISTERING RELIES ON: ATTITUDE

It depends on the belief in your ability to remember and your self-confidence that you can remember.

REGISTERING DEPENDS ON: INTEREST

What is important to remember depends on your individual interests. People of all ages, but older people especially, sort out what they are interested in remembering from what they think is unimportant. This kind of picking and choosing shuts out what you don't want to notice. You do this deliberately, and you also do so without realizing it.

REGISTERING DEPENDS ON: ATTENTION

Paying attention is the result of directing and concentrating your senses to record new information in your brain. Attitude and interest set the stage for paying attention. Attention directs your mind to something specific to the exclusion of other things. The more senses you use—seeing, hearing, touch, smell, taste—the more clearly will information be registered.

REGISTERING INVOLVES: ORGANIZING

Everyone automatically organizes new information and develops personal ways of registering it. Your brain doesn't register every detail of new information. Instead, certain details and impressions are highlighted in your memory. They are the *clues* to the rest of the information associated with them. Clues summarize the more complete and complicated information they represent.

Your brain also organizes new information to be remembered by forming associations with what you already know. This is easier to do than to remember information which has no connections for you.

An older person can find it difficult to register information for several reasons.

—He may lack self-confidence and believe that he cannot remember.

—She may be bored and have no intention of paying attention to information she considers to be trivial.

—She may be distracted and not paying attention.

—His hearing or vision may be somewhat impaired and he doesn't register accurately.

—He may have difficulty concentrating.

—She may have difficulty summarizing information into effective and appropriate clues.

—He may have difficulty linking new information with what he already knows.

✤

CHAPTER III

Storing
Your Files—
Retaining

Retaining is the process of storing information after it has been registered. A widely held theory states that short-term memory and long-term memory are two different ways of storing information.

RETAINING

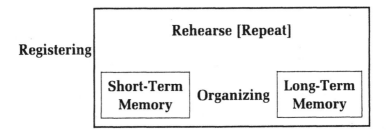

What Is Short-Term Memory?

Short-term memory has two purposes:

1. It stores items that are to be retained only briefly.
2. It also organizes information before it enters long term memory.

The ability to remember a phone number long enough to make a call is a well-known example of short-term memory.

How Does Short-Term Memory Work?

TIME SPAN IS BRIEF

You generally look up a telephone number, remember it long enough to make your call, and then probably forget it. However, if there is no answer or the line is busy, you will probably have to look up the number again.

Studies show that information in short-term memory is forgotten in approximately thirty seconds unless it is rehearsed. If this did not happen your mind would be trying to hold a lot of useless information. For example, once you have made that phone call, you probably have no need to remember the number. By forgetting it, your short-term memory makes room for taking in other information.

SHORT-TERM MEMORY IS EASILY DISRUPTED

If you focus attention on something it may enter your short-term memory, but as soon as you are distracted you are likely to forget it. For example, if you are interrupted in the middle of dialing—perhaps the doorbell rings or the soup boils over—you probably will have to look up the number again.

Another well-known example of this kind of distraction may go something like this: Perhaps you say to yourself, "I think I'll go to the fridge and get some milk." So you open the fridge door and suddenly you can't remember what you are looking for. Because getting the milk from the fridge may be a habitual act, it leaves your mind free to become preoccupied by other thoughts which quickly crowd out your thought to get the milk. Or you can also become distracted by seeing something else in the fridge which may drive out the "get the milk" thought.

Short-term memory has a very limited attention span, so when you want to hold on to information you have to try to shut out distractions.

SHORT-TERM MEMORY HAS LIMITED CAPACITY

Researchers maintain that most people can hold no more than six or seven items at once in short-term memory. For example, if you are trying to remember a particular phone number you have just looked up, along with several things you want to tell the person you are phoning, the chances are, you will be unsuccessful. The limited capacity of short-term memory determines how much information you can pay attention to at any one time.

Moving from Short-Term Memory to Long-Term Memory

REHEARSING—THE USE OF REPETITION

Going over information keeps it in short-term memory. If you were to rehearse the phone number you want to remember by saying it over and over, you probably could make your phone call later without having to look it up again. A less taxing way to keep the number in your mind is to find some kind of pattern in it.

CATEGORIZING—GROUPING

Categorizing, or organizing similar items under larger, more general headings, makes it possible to include more information in the six or seven items short-term memory can hold at any one time. Categorizing also helps to move information from short- to long-term memory. For instance, if you have many things to buy at the market you will be straining your memory to hold them all in your mind. But if you organize them under such groups as meat, vegetables, dairy products, and so on, it will be easier to remember them all. When you categorize two things happen:

—Each single item is grouped with other similar ones and they all become part of a larger unit. (Carrots, lettuce and onions are grouped under vegetables.)
—By being grouped together, individual items are organized in an orderly way which helps them

to stay in short-term memory long enough to be passed on to long-term memory. The longer information stays in short-term memory, the greater are its chances of moving into long-term memory.

In brief, short-term memory

—Receives and uses information which is quickly forgotten.
—Rehearses and organizes information which is sent on to long-term memory.

In his book, *Your Memory, How It Works and How to Improve It*, Kenneth L. Higbee uses a graphic illustration to describe these processes: "Short-term memory is like the in-basket on an office desk. Long-term memory is like the large file cabinets in the office. The in-basket has a limited capacity; it can only hold so much, then has to be emptied to make room for more. Some of what is taken out is thrown away and some is put into the file cabinets. But nothing is put into the file cabinets without first going through the in-basket."[5]

What Is Long-Term Memory?

Long-term memory is often described as being like a library, a huge filing system or storehouse of facts. This storehouse has an almost limitless capacity. The amount of information that each one of us possesses is astounding. Elizabeth Loftus, author of *Memory*, states: "It has been estimated that in a lifetime, long-term memory records as many as one quadrillion separate bits of information."[6] Hypnosis and certain drugs are able to uncover stored information from early childhood. They illustrate how deeply and permanently information can be recorded in the brain.

How Does Long-Term Memory Work?

You couldn't remember new information if it just got dumped helter-skelter into your long-term memory storehouse. It has to be organized. Organizing information starts during registering and continues during the retaining process.

Organizing clues

When you have rehearsed information in your short-term memory and are going to remember it for more than thirty seconds, you summarize and condense it. You also start to organize it in a variety of ways which link it to what you already know. As information is being transferred from short- to longer-term memory, it is being sorted out, put into categories, classified and filed systematically. Clues to the information are being formed.

HOW CLUES WORK

Clues condense information.

Your brain automatically constructs clues which condense new information so that it is easier to manage. For instance, when you have seen a two-hour movie on TV it doesn't take you the same amount of time to tell the plot to a friend. You tell it by picking out relevant highlights and identifying the important points. As you go through this process you are condensing and focussing on certain details which become your clues. They help bring back much of what you have seen.

EXAMPLES OF CLUES

Clues summarize information.

—The punchline of a joke is another example of how a clue summarizes and condenses information. When you recall it the rest of the joke's details come to mind.
—The clue "Mabel's birthday" may remind you to buy flowers, get a birthday card, arrange dinner for two at a restaurant.
—The clue "The Dust Bowl" might call up dust storms, drought, exhaustion, poverty and hard times.

Clues associate new information with what you already know.

Information is organized in different ways and in different parts of the brain. Your brain has many kinds of filing systems which can be cross referenced. Organizing makes it possible to find and use the information when you want to retrieve it from your memory.

For instance, a name can be filed by the sound of its initial letter, by the number of syllables it contains, and sometimes by its meaning. Someone's name can also be filed under such categories as where you met him or her, who else was there, and what you were doing. It can also be filed under numerous other associations. If a clue to one set of associations does not work, you try another and another. Clue by clue and piece by piece you reconstruct the information you are searching. There are countless kinds of associations available in your long-term memory.

**Everyone forms his or her
own individual clues.**

The ability to make effective clues varies from person to person, age to age and situation to situation. People who are poor at remembering jokes, for example, may have excellent abilities to organize clues for remembering other things. They may be good at remembering the plot of a book, names and faces, how to repair an electrical appliance. Their memory for directions may be good. Once they have been to a place they know how to get there again. People are very individual in their use of the clues which help them to remember.

**"When you remember a fresh piece
of information you automatically
process the information. A fact never
simply arrives and takes up residence!"[7]**

CLUES

—Condense information.

—Summarize information.

—Associate new information with what you already know.

Everyone forms his or her own individual clues.

General Knowledge Memory and Personal Experience Memory

Psychologists talk about two parts of long-term memory, General Knowledge Memory and Personal Experience Memory.[8]

GENERAL KNOWLEDGE MEMORY

General Knowledge Memory deals with your knowledge of the world based on your understanding of words and ideas, such as knowing that there is a continent called Europe, that some buildings are called houses while others are called apartments, that a kilometer is 5/8 of a mile, that bananas and oranges are fruit, etc. General Knowledge Memory stores all the knowledge you need to be able to use language, to be logical, to solve problems, to express yourself and to understand what others are saying. It stores the factual, impersonal knowledge you have learned throughout your life.

PERSONAL EXPERIENCE MEMORY

Personal Experience Memory stores all the happenings and occurrences, big and small, that make up your own life history. It stores everything from memories of your first day in school to the most important moment in your life; memories of joy and sorrow, good times, bad times, and everything in between. It records whom you met yesterday and under what circumstances, what you had to eat today, what you are going to do tomorrow and next month.

Personal Experience Memory brings together all the sense impressions and emotions that provide the continuity of your life. It records all the changes and happenings that make up your inner and outer worlds and that add up to who you are, what you do, day after day. Because it records a constant flow of change, personal experience memory does not hold on to many of the details that enter it. General Knowledge Memory, on the other hand, tends to be more stable.

With increasing age the remembering difficulties of older people are frequently those of recent Personal Experience Memory. Their General Knowledge Memory and Personal Experience Memory from the past are relatively more trustworthy.

Here are some examples of General Knowledge and Personal Experience Memory. Test yourself to see which questions are easy to answer and which are not.

✔ TEST YOUR GENERAL KNOWLEDGE MEMORY

1. In what directions does the sun rise and set?
2. Who was the first President of the United States?
3. Name one of the ingredients in cheese.

4. What is the name of the film starring Clark Gable and Vivien Leigh dealing with the American Civil War?
5. How many feet are in a mile?

✔ TEST YOUR PERSONAL EXPERIENCE MEMORY

1. When did you last dine out, and with whom?
2. What was the first spanking or punishment you remember as a child? What was it for?
3. How did you first hear about the Wall Street Crash of 1929?
4. What did you have for lunch last Tuesday?
5. Who called you on the telephone yesterday and what did he/she have to say?

Did You Notice:

1. Which questions took longer to answer—those from your general knowledge or from your personal experience memory?
2. Which questions required some thought?
3. Which questions you answered automatically?

These quizzes show that some material in your General Knowledge Memory is well organized and stable through being rehearsed over a long period of time. Information from your recent Personal Experience Memory may not have been so easy to retrieve because you have had less opportunity to rehearse it (as in question 5), or no particular reason to rehearse it (as in question 4). In contrast, it is often easy to recall information from your early life, because it has been well organized, rehearsed many times, and, as past history, is stable and unchanged.

Answers to General Knowledge Quiz

The theories of short-term memory and long-term memory have been developed to explain how people store information. Although there are other theories about retaining, at present the short-term memory–long-term memory ones seem to explain retaining best.

Retaining— Summary

Retaining is the process of storing information after it has been registered. Retaining makes use of two different memory stores—*Short-Term Memory* and *Long-Term Memory*.

WHAT IS SHORT-TERM MEMORY?

Short-term memory:
1. Receives and uses information which is then quickly forgotten.
2. Rehearses and organizes information which is sent on to long-term memory.

SHORT-TERM MEMORY IS BRIEF

Information in short-term memory is forgotten in approximately thirty seconds unless it is rehearsed. An example of short-term memory is the ability to hang on to a new phone number long enough to make a call.

SHORT-TERM MEMORY IS EASILY DISRUPTED

Concentrating on something allows it to enter your short-term memory. But if you are distracted by something else, the original information can easily be forgotten.

SHORT-TERM MEMORY CAPACITY IS LIMITED

Most people can hold about six or seven items at once in their short-term memory. This limited capacity determines how much information you can pay attention to at any one time. You can increase your short-term memory capacity by categorizing items to be remembered and then organizing them into groups.

MOVING FROM SHORT-TERM MEMORY
TO LONG-TERM MEMORY

Rehearsing, or going over information, keeps it in short-term memory. The longer information stays in short-term memory the greater are its chances of moving to long-term memory. As information is being transferred from short- to long-term memory it is being organized, categorized and filed systematically. It is being linked, through many associations, to knowledge already in long-term memory.

WHAT IS LONG-TERM MEMORY?

Long-term memory is described as a huge filing system or storehouse of facts. It has almost limitless capacity.

ORGANIZING THE STORAGE OF
INFORMATION IN LONG-TERM MEMORY

You couldn't recall information if it were dumped into your long-term memory storehouse without any order. Clues help to organize information.

CLUES

Continuing the process started in short-term memory, your brain condenses and summarizes new information into manageable pieces called clues.
Clues form links with what you already know.
When you recall a clue it helps to recall other details that are associated with it.
You organize clues to new information in many different ways and in different parts of your brain.
You make countless associations between new information and what you already know.

LONG-TERM MEMORY HAS TWO PARTS:
GENERAL KNOWLEDGE MEMORY
AND PERSONAL EXPERIENCE MEMORY

General Knowledge Memory stores factual impersonal knowledge that you have learned throughout your life. It stores all the knowledge you need to have to be able to use language, to be logical, to solve problems, to express yourself and to understand what others are saying.

Personal Experience Memory stores all the events, big and small, that make up your personal life history—who you are and what you do. It records a constant flow of change. Because of this, Personal Experience Memory is more subject to forgetting than is General Knowledge Memory.

Finding the Needle in the Haystack— Retrieving

Retrieving is the process of finding and pulling out information you have registered and stored in your long-term memory.

RETRIEVING

Recognition Recall

Retrieving consists of *recall* and *recognition*. *Recall* requires searching your memory for specific information and then producing it. *Recognition* requires matching information that is presented to you with what you already know. In most cases, recall is more difficult than recognition, and when someone says "I can't

remember," he usually means that he cannot recall
something.

Recall requires:
1) Searching the memory for information.
2) Producing it.

Most of the time you retrieve information so quickly
that the process seems automatic—you never give it
a thought. It is only when you run into retrieval snags
that you are aware of how you must search to find
what you are looking for.

The "Tip of the Tongue" Experience

Your brain contains tremendous amounts of information, some of which cannot be tapped and retrieved
at any given moment. Although the information is
stored, you may feel as though you are looking for a
needle in a haystack. You know it is there but you
cannot put your finger on it.

When you are having difficulty recalling the name
of someone you know, you are frequently having a
"tip of the tongue" experience. You know that the
person's name is in your memory but it isn't available.
You may be able to picture the person in your mind's
eye, or remember some part of his or her name or a
name like it, or the rhythm or general sound of the
name. Or you can remember other information about
the person, such as where you met, whose friend he or
she is, etc. You are *almost* able to recall the name, but

not quite. Finally, you say "It's on the tip of my tongue" because you know you have the knowledge stored. You are trying all your clues and associations, but you still cannot retrieve it.

"Go and retrieve!"

An internal monitor appears to operate as you search the pathways of associations to the information you are seeking. This monitor seems to say, "Go and retrieve. If you do not find what you are looking for down one pathway, try another and another, until you do find it."

The search might go something like this: "Now what is the name of that woman with the curly hair who is the friend of Mrs. Smith ... who I met either at church, or was it at the club when Polly Green introduced her to me? I think her name begins with R, or is it B? Mrs. Rooster? No, that couldn't be—Mrs. Brewster? Yes, that's it! And her first name, is it biblical? —Sarah, Rebecca, Judith? No, none of these. Try the New Testament. Elizabeth, Martha, Mary? I'm getting close. It's Mary something. Mary Anne, Mary Elizabeth? Oh wait, it's the same as my granddaughter's— Rosemary. No, not quite, but it does have a flower in it. Ah, it's Mary Rose—Mary Rose Brewster. At last!"

The monitor will recognize what you are looking for and will discard information which doesn't fit. However, from time to time it may get stuck on a word which closely resembles the one you are seeking. For example, the name you want is "Mary Rose" but the one that keeps popping up in your head is "Rosemary," your granddaughter's name. You may have

43

difficulty retrieving "Mary Rose" because it is so strongly blocked by "Rosemary."

But the monitor will continue working on an unconscious level long after you have given up trying, and often the correct name will suddenly appear. It can seem amazing to wake in the middle of the night remembering a name you have been looking for earlier that day. Everyone has experienced the delight and sense of relief when, after a long search, the information you are seeking seems to pop into your head.

THE WEB OF ASSOCIATIONS

The tip of the tongue experience suggests that something you are looking for in long-term memory is usually just not where you expected it to be. The name you want is organized and stored in many ways, surrounded by a web of associations. To retrieve it you will need to find the clues to the associations that will lead you to the name itself.

The fact that you have been circling around the name, picking up different clues that tell you something about it, indicates that people remember information in pieces. Though you often remember only part of something, through a series of clues you can reach more and more of what has been stored. Key words, sights, smells, sounds, tastes are all clues.

The next time you have a "tip of the tongue" experience, give yourself a few moments to go through the clues you used to recall the information you were seeking. Not only is this pleasant and reassuring, it helps to anchor the information in your memory more securely. Another time you might not have to repeat the agony of searching for it again.

Recognition

Why is it easier to recognize a person's face than to recall his or her name?

"Your face is familiar, but
I can't recall your name."

In recall you must first locate all the information required for producing the name, and then supply it. In recognition, on the other hand, information is presented to you and you then decide if it fits with what you already know. For example, you might glance at someone and think, "I know Mary Rose Brewster. She's the curly-haired woman over there with the plump face and blue eyes. I can link her appearance with her name. On the other hand, that dark-haired thin-faced woman with the bun at the back of her head does not look at all like Mary Rose, so she must be someone else."

The dictionary defines *recognize* as "to know again; perceive as identical with someone or something previously known." Because recognition requires you to choose among a limited number of alternatives it is generally easier than recall.

The following Recall and Recognition Quiz demonstrates the different demands that are made on the memory. The quiz asks each question twice. First you are asked to recall the answer. Then you are asked to recognize the answer.

✔ RECALL

Answer the following:

1. Who played Dorothy in *The Wizard of Oz*?
2. Who was Prime Minister of England during World War II?
3. Who was the first black player in major league baseball?
4. Who was Popeye's girlfriend?
5. What important German official flew to Great Britain during World War II?

✔ RECOGNITION

Circle the letter of the correct answer to the following questions:

1. Who played Dorothy in *The Wizard of Oz*?
   a) Shirley Temple b) Mitzi Gaynor c) Debbie Reynolds d) Judy Garland
2. Who was Prime Minister of England during World War II?
   a) Neville Chamberlain b) Clement R. Attlee c) Winston Churchill d) Anthony Eden
3. Who was the first black player in major league baseball?
   a) Joe E. Brown b) Jackie Robinson c) Joe Lewis d) Willy Mays
4. Who was Popeye's girlfriend?
   a) Blondie b) Betty Boop c) Nancy d) Olive Oyl
5. What important German official flew to Great Britain during World War II?
   a) Charles de Gaulle b) Rudolf Hess c) Alger Hiss d) Albert Speers

ANSWERS

THE FIVE SENSES AND RECOGNITION

Other senses besides vision are also extremely important in recognition. Your sense of hearing allows you to recognize "Happy Birthday," or your grandchild's voice. Your sense of smell allows you to recognize the odor of the perfume your mother used to wear, or to know that the cookies in the oven are done. Your sense of touch recognizes warm sand under your feet, or an itchy sweater. Your sense of taste recognizes a chocolate cake or "turned" butter.

You recognize countless things every day through using your senses, and you normally take them for granted. But if some senses become less acute you begin to appreciate the full extent of their importance, realizing how precious they are as the means of keeping in touch with the world.

Retrieval through recall and recognition is the end result of a threefold process:

1. Registering information well.
2. Storing it efficiently.
3. Finding it when you need it.

47

Retrieving—Summary

Retrieving is the process of getting information from your memory after it has been registered and stored. Retrieving consists of recall and recognition.

RECALL

In the process of recalling something, you search your memory for the specific information you want, and when it is found you produce it. Recall depends on how well you have organized the information you are looking for—how many clues you have formed and how many associations those clues have with other information you have stored.

The experience of searching your memory to find information that you know is there but can't quite grasp is known as the "tip of the tongue" experience. Information in long term memory which seems to be lost is not filed where it is expected to be. To retrieve it, correct clues need to be found.

Key words, sights, smells, sounds, tastes, are all clues. Clues point out pathways of associations, prompting you to search out information you are looking for.

RECOGNITION

When you recognize something you decide if the information you are presented fits with what you are seeking. This is usually an easier process than the process of recall. In recall you have to start from scratch to hunt for clues. In recognition you are given the clues and you have to decide if they are the correct ones. Your senses play a big part in recognition.

You recognize countless things every day through using your senses.

**RETRIEVAL THROUGH RECALL AND
RECOGNITION IS THE END RESULT
OF A THREE-FOLD PROCESS:**

1. Registering information well.
2. Storing it efficiently.
3. Finding it when it is needed.

CHAPTER V

Why We Forget

What did you do on June 2, 1978? What did you eat for lunch last Thursday? What were the newspaper headlines two days ago? Unless there is a good reason to remember, most people forget this kind of information.

If you did not forget, your mind would be swamped with useless information and unable to handle the demands of your daily life. Much forgetting is natural and necessary. It is the result of sorting out what is meaningful and useful, and it keeps your mind clear to store needed information.

Forgetting can occur in many ways and for many reasons. Absentmindedness is a common type of forgetting.

Absentmindedness

When someone's mind is "absent" through preoccupation with other thoughts, he or she fails to register information. This kind of forgetting is different from the inability to recall, in which information is registered and stored. People of all ages differ in their proneness to absentmindedness, but as a person gets older, absentmindedness tends to become more pronounced. It most often occurs in the following circumstances:

1. When you are in surroundings that are familiar to you.
2. When you are doing something habitual and automatic, requiring little attention or concentration.
3. When your mind is distracted or preoccupied but you are not under great stress from the outside.[9]

"I have made lists since I was 17."

Absentmindedness is also partly the result of the kind of personality you have, not just your age. Someone who is preoccupied and who pays little attention to detail may have been that way all his life. But as he grows older, his absentmindedness will probably increase. The opposite of the "absentminded professor" is the person who is aware of every little thing and plans down to the last detail. He is much less likely to forget because he has trained himself all his life to pay attention to details and to use memory aids such as lists, calendars, and so on. As he grows older, he may develop more ways to avoid forgetting. Most people fall between these two extremes.

If absentmindedness is mainly the result of not paying attention, the way to reduce it is to put more conscious energy into the act of registering. For example, if losing track of your glasses is a problem, it is a good idea to say aloud to yourself as you put them down, "I am putting my glasses down here." Then tell yourself, "I had better look at them and really notice what I am doing." There is no cure for absentmindedness, other than finding better ways to highlight the act of paying attention.

Disuse Theory

There is a theory which states that time and disuse may affect memory. Forgetting happens over time and memories simply fade away. For example, many people have slight recollections of something they once learned at school, but with disuse the recollection seems to become dimmer and dimmer. This theory seems to make sense, but it is only a partial explanation of why people forget.

Interference Theory

Another theory states that some kinds of forgetting are caused by interference in your filing system. The giant storage cabinet in long term memory starts out with relatively few files in it. When you were six or eight years old you might have had several thousand stored away. By the time you have reached the age of sixty-six or sixty-eight, you may have several billion files. Finding the right one was a lot easier when you were six than it is when you are sixty-six. With a far less sophisticated filing system, the six-year-old does not have so many chances of running into interferences. However, as you age, interference becomes more significant. If some of the newer files in your system are similar to older ones, you can experience difficulties in retrieving the right one. This happens, for instance, when you search for a name, such as Mary Rose, and you get stuck on the name Rosemary. Memories connect with one another and often run into each other.

Interference can occur when something you know blocks something new you are trying to learn or remember. If you once learned French, you may find that as you study another language, a French word pops into your mind while you grope for the word in the second language. Or knowing where you used to store utensils in your old kitchen may interfere with remembering where you have now put them in your new kitchen.

Interference can also occur when new information gets in the way of information already in your memory. The events of last week may interfere with your memory of the events of last month. You can remember whom you met on the street yesterday, but not whom you met last November.

Distorted Memory

"We fill up the lowlands of
our memories from the highlands
of our imaginations."[10]

Almost all memories involve some forgetting. You always select from an experience the events and impressions that seem important to you, and no two people remember in exactly the same way. A memory depends on who is doing the remembering. The memory of an incident or something you have witnessed is bound to be colored by your feelings and understanding. You might unconsciously change details to be more in line with your wishes, or what you think makes sense. Selective remembering often happens when people think of the "good old days."

Sometimes people misunderstand what they hear or see and the information gets misfiled. For instance, seeing a man with a dagger in his hand could be interpreted in several ways:

—He is about to kill someone.
—He is about to kill himself.
—He discovered someone killed and has just removed the blade.
—He has a dagger collection and is examining this one.

How you file this information will depend on how you initially interpret it.

Information that is not filed appropriately is often very difficult to retrieve because you keep looking in the wrong place. For example, searching for your parked car can be extremely frustrating when you are sure that you are looking in the right place and in fact you have actually parked the car somewhere else.

Repression

Sigmund Freud claimed that we push memories that cause anxiety and are unpleasant or unacceptable out of our conscious minds. By repressing these negative memories we do not have to deal with them directly. We all repress memories to a certain extent because feelings about events affect how we remember them.

Summary

There are many valid reasons for forgetting, especially as we grow older. Preoccupations, distractions, feelings, and possibly disuse, all affect the ability to remember. Interference increases because we are all owners of highly sophisticated and well stocked filing systems. It is no wonder that we get lost from time to time.

CHAPTER VI

Am I Losing My Grip? Aging and Memory

Introduction

This chapter discusses individual differences in normal memory changes among older adults. It also discusses the effects of changing energy levels and changing pace on memory.

The chapter explores abnormal changes in remembering caused by brain disorders, including Alzheimer's disease. It points out that certain memory problems can be successfully treated, and emphasizes that serious brain disorders affect only a very small number of older adults. The effects of depression on memory are also considered, and the distinction is made between normal sadness and clinical depression.

Finally, this chapter looks at intelligence and learning in later life. Although the pace of older people may be slower, their capacity to learn and grow still remains and can flourish. Seniors have unique opportunities to use their experience and wisdom to develop old and new interests and talents, to use their minds to keep active, alert, and engaged with life.

We Are All Individuals

STEREOTYPES

There is a tendency to speak of "the elderly" or "senior citizens" as though they were a group of people who are all the same. Like any other age group, older people do share basic human needs and common problems. But, as in any other age group, there are large individual differences among seniors.

When people are lumped together, certain stereotyped expectations are set up about how they will behave. Accordingly, old people are expected to be set in their ways and rigid in their thinking, forgetful, absentminded, and sometimes confused. They may also be seen as inadequate in dealing with life because they are slower to respond to what is going on around them.

These stereotypes fail to recognize that there are differences between people in their 60's and 70's and those in their 80's and 90's. They also fail to recognize that there are great differences among individuals within all these age categories.

Stereotyping older people creates a myth which says that to be old is to be a lesser human being. Stereotypes emphasize eccentricity, ill health, poverty, and loneliness. Unfortunately, some seniors accept this view of themselves. But most older adults see through the myth and reject it, recognizing that it is merely an oversimplified half-truth.

Ability and interest don't "turn off" at a given age.

Aging need not be equated with disease or deterioration. Ability and interest don't "turn off" at a given age. Many older people lead active and fulfilling lives. They pursue interesting and creative activities and are deeply involved in their community, friends and family. Older adults have opportunities to use the breadth of their experience and wisdom to enrich themselves and others. One of the challenges facing older people is to help the rest of society to see seniors for who they really are—older individuals.

THE SUM OF YOUR EXPERIENCES

With age each person becomes increasingly different from others as he becomes more himself. Changes in appearance reflect important internal changes, both emotional and intellectual, that happen to everyone throughout a lifetime. Each person carries within himself the sum of his own experiences—early childhood, family, schooling and friendships; work, responsibilities, achievements and failures; frustrations, ordeals, joys and satisfactions. As people mature, some become more self-confident and others more self-effacing. Some people have plumbed the depths and experienced the heights, while others have known more stable, balanced lives. Breadth or narrowness of experience has played its roles in shaping an individual. By the time someone is in her mature years she can truly say "I am a unique person."

"I am a unique person."

The memory and intellectual changes that occur with aging are as varied as the physical and emotional ones. Therefore it is difficult to make specific statements about memory changes in aging that apply with equal validity to *all* older people. Memory changes do occur, but they do so at different ages, different rates, and with different intensity for each person. Information about the memory functioning of the "average" older person may have some value, but it does not necessarily describe any particular individual.

Memory and Energy Levels

As we get older, all of us have to consider the energy we can invest in activities, including the activity of remembering.

ENERGY LEVELS AFFECT:

—Attitudes and moods—our interest and desire to remember and confidence in our ability to remember.

—Attention—our level of awareness and ability to concentrate.

—Ability to organize new information by sorting and linking it to what we already know so that it can be stored.

—Ability to retrieve information from our memories, either by recalling it or recognizing it.

If we no longer have what used to seem like an unlimited amount of energy, we naturally become more selective about how we spend it. Because we have to work harder to remember, we tend to let things slip by that we previously might have made an effort to remember.

**We become more selective
about how we spend our energy.**

Our energy levels are sufficient to handle our affairs well when things are running smoothly. However, energy levels can drop at certain times, when people are tired, ill, depressed or upset. These times can occur at any stage of life, of course, but they are more likely to happen as people age.

CONCENTRATION AND DISTRACTIBILITY

Concentration, which is central to remembering, uses energy in a very specific way. To pay attention, people need to focus their energy. Recognizing a tendency toward distractibility, many older adults are able to direct their energy and develop skills to concentrate more consciously and deliberately than they did when they were younger.

Some older people complain about their lessening ability to concentrate. They become easily distracted, unable to direct their attention as well or as long as they once did. "Wool gathering," worries, the state of their bodies, put claims on their attention. Sounds,

61

sights, and disruptions from the outside may also intrude and divert their attention.

Studies show that most older people have some difficulty holding in mind different sets of information that they hear at the same time. An example of this is being caught in the cross fire of two different conversations going on around you. Older people experience more interference, and are less able than younger people to divide their attention. To avoid this overload, many older adults learn to deal with things one at a time.

**Many older adults learn to
deal with things one at a time.**

CHANGING PACE

Each person has a different rate of changing pace, both physically and mentally. There is no set time at which we are "supposed" to change pace and begin to slow down, but inevitably we do. Nevertheless, we still continue to do many of the things we have always done—pay attention, solve problems, and reason, although the time it takes to do them may change.

It would be less than human not to regret the slowing down of our memory processes. As we compare ourselves with younger people, or even more important, with ourselves at a younger age, it is easy to feel that we have lost something valuable. Forgetting can be frustrating, but it is not necessarily a sign of falling apart at the seams. People who accept the slower pace of their memory processes, as they do the slowing down in their bodies, avoid wasted energy in worry and distress over what is the natural course of things.

Senility and Brain Disorders

Many people, young and old, believe that it is inevitable as people grow older they become senile—increasingly confused, disoriented and forgetful. This belief is not based on fact. A very small percentage of older people actually become senile, or brain impaired. Here are approximate percentages:

1. Ninety-five percent of people sixty-five and older are **not** senile.
2. Ninety percent of people in their seventies and over are **not** affected by brain impairment.
3. Even in the population of people in their eighties, eighty percent are mentally unimpaired. The incidence of brain disorders appears to level out after the age of eighty-five.[11]

A very small percentage of older people suffer from Alzheimer's disease.

It cannot be emphasized enough that AGING IN ITSELF IS NOT A DISEASE. If people suddenly become confused, or have large memory gaps, they are likely to be suffering from a specific condition. Sudden confusion and loss of memory are symptoms of that condition, just as a high temperature might be a symptom of a baby's sore throat or earache. They are not a part of the normal aging process.

WHAT IS SENILITY?

Senility is a catchword that has been used for many years. It explains very little and has often been used to label any eccentric behavior of an older person. Sometimes senility has been equated with such terms as "chronic brain failure," "chronic brain syndrome," "organic brain syndrome," and "senile dementia." Senility is also equated with Alzheimer's disease.

It is now believed that 50–60% of those older people whose brains are impaired suffer from Alzheimer's disease. Approximately 20–25% of brain impairment is caused by strokes, and the remainder is the result of other causes.[12] If a person is showing the symptoms of forgetfulness, confusion, and disorientation, it is necessary to determine if these symptoms are the result of a specific condition. This is much more useful and humane than simply labelling him or her "senile."

Senility is a catchword.

OTHER COMMON CAUSES FOR CONFUSION, DISORIENTATION, AND FORGETFULNESS

A number of reasons for confusion, forgetfulness, and disorientation are caused by conditions other than Alzheimer's disease. They are treatable! It is important to check out the cause of these symptoms. People who *appear* to have Alzheimer's disease may actually be affected by any of the following problems:

1. *Overmedication or medication interactions*—too

many prescription or non-prescription drugs, or a combination of both.

2. *Chemical imbalances in the body*—not enough potassium, an abnormal thyroid, or abnormal blood sugar level.

3. *Depression*—feelings of worthlessness, helplessness, and despair.

4. *Sudden illness*—bacterial infections, flu, pneumonia.

5. *Malnutrition and dehydration*—inadequate diet and not enough fluid in the body.

6. *Social isolation*—living conditions, poverty, illness, and emotional problems.

With proper care and treatment all of these situations can be reversed. If these or similar problems do not explain forgetting and confusion, Alzheimer's disease is suspected.[13]

WHAT IS ALZHEIMER'S DISEASE?

In Alzheimer's disease, brain cells slowly deteriorate and mental functioning gradually declines. At the beginning the person with Alzheimer's may not be able to remember recent events, names, appointments, and so on. As the disease progresses, he becomes increasingly confused about his immediate environment, about directions, about time and even normal daily routines. He forgets important events entirely, and not just the details. He cannot learn new information, solve problems, or make decisions. His personality may change significantly.

Diagnosis of Alzheimer's disease is usually done by a process of elimination. It is therefore crucial not to label someone as having Alzheimer's disease without

65

a thorough diagnosis, even though he or she may appear confused, disoriented, and forgetful. At this point in Alzheimer's research, the only way the disease can be diagnosed with complete certainty is by examining the brain after death.

Although the cause of Alzheimer's disease is not known yet, and at present it cannot be cured, much research is being conducted and many new areas are being explored.

✔ COMMON AND ABNORMAL FORGETTING

This quiz may help you sort out whether your forgetting is fairly usual, or whether it is an indication of something which requires attention.

Answer "Yes" or "No" to the following statements. *Most of the time* you can't remember:

1. where you put your keys.
2. where you were born.
3. the name of your neighbor whom you meet on the street.
4. to pay your rent.
5. where you parked your car.
6. where you put important papers.

Normal reasons for forgetting, such as absentmindedness, fatigue, illness or sadness, might make you answer "yes" to numbers 1, 3, and 5. However, when you consistently cannot remember such items as numbers 2, 4, and 6, you may have a more significant problem which should be checked by your physician.[14]

THESE IMPORTANT FACTS ABOUT ALZHEIMER'S
DISEASE ARE WORTH REPEATING

1. It is very difficult to diagnose Alzheimer's disease accurately, especially in its early stages.
2. Since an accurate diagnosis is so difficult, it should be done with great care.
3. It is crucial not to automatically label someone who appears confused, disoriented, and forgetful as having Alzheimer's disease. The person's problems may be treatable and reversible.

If forgetting becomes a constant problem to you or someone close to you, it is wise to get a physical checkup. Or check with your local Alzheimer's Support Association.

Depression and Memory

The word "depression" means different things to different people. Some people call it "being down in the dumps" or "feeling blue." Others use the term to describe a deep sadness, which most people have experienced at some time in their lives. But neither of these is what doctors mean when they refer to clinical depression.

NORMAL SADNESS

Older people are especially vulnerable to events that can lead to depression. If you have lost a person close to you, developed a physical condition that curtails your activities, or moved from familiar surroundings, it is normal and appropriate to feel sad. In fact, it is healthy to grieve for loss and change. Grief is hard but necessary work. It allows a person to make a healthy adjustment to the changes which have occurred. Feelings of sadness and grief generally pass with time.

SYMPTOMS OF DEPRESSION

Clinical or true depression is not the same as sadness and grief. It is a condition in which a person thinks and feels that he or she is powerless, worthless, and hopeless. These feelings may develop from an accumulation of losses that become overwhelming. They go beyond normal grieving.

The behavior of a truly depressed person changes and may move toward extremes. He or she either begins to overeat or hardly eats at all. Such a person gets little sleep or sleeps all the time. Depressed people lack energy, are listless, and often become apathetic and socially withdrawn. Their thoughts, movements, and behavior slow down. It can be very difficult for a person to break out of this psychological paralysis.

A number of depressed people do not admit having feelings of depression. Instead, they express their depression by complaining about physical ailments such as headaches, constipation, or upset stomach.

MEMORY AND DEPRESSION

Depression has a marked effect on an individual's thinking and reasoning abilities, and depressed people have memory problems. They have trouble remembering recent events and sometimes even past events. One day their memory may work well and the next day it may not. They have difficulties concentrating and paying attention, and can feel confused and bewildered. They may ramble and find it difficult to keep to a topic. It is easy to mistake these symptoms for Alzheimer's disease, or dismiss them as everyday problems of the aged. In fact, such memory problems may be due to a serious depression which can be treated. A competent and thorough diagnosis is essential.

BEING WITH A DEPRESSED PERSON

Being with a depressed person can be very difficult and stressful. From time to time it may be necessary for the one who is caring for a depressed person to take a break. It is important for that person to seek such an outlet without feeling guilty.

Many people tend to draw away from someone who is depressed. This can lead to even greater isolation for the depressed person. Depression, in any case, tends to feed on itself, and someone afflicted with it can sink deeper and deeper into inactivity and feelings of hopelessness unless he or she gets help.

DEALING WITH DEPRESSION

If, from time to time, you feel depressed, here are some suggestions to help you.

1. Share your problems with a friend.
2. Be open about your feelings; let people know that you are hurting and vulnerable. Denying your feelings takes a lot of energy and will increase your distress.
3. Try to set aside a specific time to give in to your feelings. Give expression to anger, frustration, self-blame and blame of others. It may seem artificial,

but if you can choose where and with whom you are going to do this, you will find it helpful. But don't go on endlessly. This will just feed your negative emotions.

4. Do something physical to get yourself moving, even if you feel tired or not in the mood. Choose an enjoyable activity such as walking, jogging, swimming, working in the garden, or even doing spring housecleaning. Make yourself move. Physical activity can help lift your mood.

5. Do something nice for yourself—buy yourself a gift, take a holiday, visit a friend. Treat yourself as you would someone who is very dear and special to you.

6. Do something that needs to be done and which also has a reward attached to it. Sometimes accomplishing a task that you've postponed, such as writing a letter or cleaning out some drawers, will help counteract the feelings of depression.

If you still have difficulties, outside help is available. Consult your doctor, or call your local Mental Health Association.

By no means does aging always involve changes which suggest serious decline in memory. As we explore intelligence and learning it is clear that adults have a great capacity to remain mentally active and alert, to learn and grow in later life.

Intelligence and Aging

For a long time it was thought that a person's intelligence declined with age. Some researchers even went so far as to state that an adult reached his peak of intellectual capacity at age twenty-six, after which his intelligence steadily decreased over the years. Researchers reached this conclusion by testing university students in their early twenties and people over the age of sixty and comparing their IQ scores. Those over sixty did less well than the younger people. This reinforced the belief that intelligence declined as people got older.

One explanation for the poorer performance of older adults came from their having grown up in a different era with different experiences and education from the university students with whom they were compared. The older people's opportunities to develop and explain certain aspects of their intellectual potential had been limited. Many of the earlier generation had gone to work at age fourteen or sixteen in physically demanding jobs. They had little energy left for other activities. There was no television, and there were fewer publications. For some people there was less access to books, lectures, concerts, theatre, and other cultural activities.

Eventually, researchers began to question whether they had been making fair comparisons. Had these older adults been brighter when they were age twenty-five? Would these younger people being tested lose some of their intellectual capacities later on? In a new study, psychologists observed the same adults for forty years, from their twenties to their sixties, testing them every ten years. They found that there was little decline in overall general intelligence. With each test the adults' scores remained almost the same, decade after decade.

In tests involving speed of reaction and recognition,

the scores of older adults are usually lower than those of younger people. But timed or speed-related tests can cause considerable anxiety, especially in older people, and interfere with learning and remembering. However, in tests which measure knowledge, experience, problem solving, reasoning, and vocabulary, older adults do as well as and at times even better than young people.

The results of the tests suggest that the store of knowledge increases with age. The ability to solve problems and to reason does not diminish—it may actually increase. However, older people need a more leisurely pace to deal comfortably with new information and new situations.

The notion that older people are not as intelligent as younger ones is simply untrue.

Learning and Aging

Learning new information and new behavior at any age is part of growing. Learning adds to the quality of life, making it more interesting and satisfying. Registering, retaining and retrieving all influence the way people learn.

The capacity to learn does not decrease as people grow older. However, mood, self-confidence, and desire deeply affect the ability to learn. Older people do not waste their time and energy on things which do not interest them. They are more sharply aware of what is important and become more selective. Conserving energy and dwelling on what is interesting, gives pleasure, or is useful become increasingly important.

Research has shown that some people tend to see themselves as more forgetful than they actually are. When this is the case they tend to be unsure of themselves when faced with learning new things. If someone believes that he cannot learn because he is too old, his belief can become a self-fulfilling prophecy. But older people learn well when they are presented with new ideas and experiences at a pace which is suitable to them. They use their intelligence and life experience very effectively.

The big difference between the way in which young and old people learn is that older people take more time to register and store information, search for it, and recall it.

CONDITIONS FOR SUCCESSFUL LEARNING

Here are some conditions which help older people to learn successfully:

1. Insure that your surroundings are pleasant and relaxed.
2. Allow plenty of uninterrupted time.
3. Allow yourself opportunities for asking questions, either of others or of yourself.
4. Deal only with as much as you can comfortably handle.
5. Follow short periods of concentration with brief periods of rest.
6. Practice and repeat the information.
7. Make learning fun. Enjoy yourself!

These conditions for successful learning do not apply only to older adults. People of all ages learn better under the same conditions. Children and young adults often do not have any control over their learning environments. Fortunately, older people usually have a choice.

There is a particular satisfaction when you are older in learning new things and in having time to expand knowledge and develop skills you already possess. Many older people feel that their lives are greatly enriched by learning, either by themselves or with others. The life of the mind, the pleasure of growing and discovering, can be one of the joys of age.

The satisfactions and pleasures of learning in later life are discussed by John A. B. McLeish, an older adult himself, in his book, *The Ulyssean Adult— Creativity in the Middle and Later Years.*

PART II

Dealing With Memory Changes

CHAPTER VII

Common Practical Strategies for Remembering in Everyday Situations

Introduction

The normal change in pace which occurs as people age usually affects the efficiency of their memories. Remembering details becomes more difficult. Many people deal with this by lessening the demands made on their memories. How an individual lives plays a big part in these demands. One person may lead a quiet life, with regular routines. Another may live a much more active and complicated life. The busy person will probably find it harder to remember things because he is juggling so many details in his head. People on the run often rely on diaries, calendars, lists, timers, and other memory aids which take away the burden of trying to remember a lot of details.

This chapter has been compiled from information gathered from books, personal experiences, and mainly from discussions with many older adults. The suggestions can help you to remember a variety of practical details in everyday situations. They are all effective and easy to use, and all are based on the principles of registering, retaining and retrieving. And, as in all memory matters, they rely on attitude and attention. Your attitude and attention will help determine how well you remember something.

Accentuate the Positive

One senior remarked that you have to put some energy into remembering. It takes some effort. Another added that a positive attitude will go a long way toward supplying that energy. They are both talking about motivation, which is where it all starts. You can remember more efficiently if you think that doing so is worthwhile.

Many people say "I learned the hard way" to remember where they put keys, glasses, dentures, or what have you. Being taught the hard way is painful. Everyone has particular things that are especially frustrating to forget. When this happens, don't panic. It is important to let go, relax and take a philosophic attitude. As you take the pressure off, what you are searching for may well pop into your mind.

PAY ATTENTION

"Ah yes," you may say. "If only I could or would pay attention most of my memory troubles would disappear." And you are probably right. Paying attention requires concentration. Sometimes that is not easy.

The following strategies can help to make your memory more efficient for dealing with the demands of daily living. They will not make you a memory whiz, but they will help where it really counts—in matters that affect you on a daily basis. Some strategies are tried and true old chestnuts. Others may be just the new angles you have been looking for.

☞ Strategy #1: Be Organized

MAKING LISTS

Where would we be if we couldn't make lists? They ease us through many of life's challenges, from "What do I need at the market?" to "What exactly is in my safe deposit box?" to scheduling repair jobs around the house. Lists are portable memory aids.

To use them to best advantage:

1. Lists should be kept in one place where you can easily find them.
2. Lists should be on big pieces of paper so they are easy to see and read.
3. Long lists should be organized into categories.

ORGANIZING YOUR SHOPPING LIST

To make your shopping list work best for you, organize it into groups or categories such as meat, vegetables, fruit, dairy products, canned goods, staples, etc. Categorizing items helps you get everything you need. It is also easier to check items off in each group than it is to run your eye down a long list of unrelated items.

ORGANIZING A LIST OF
WHAT TO TAKE ON A TRIP

Contents of a suitcase or trunk can be listed under categories. Some suggestions for organizing clothing are to start with footwear and move up the body; or start with inner wear and go to outer wear; or group clothes by night wear, casual clothes, dressy clothes. Try your own categories. Medications, toiletries, special equipment, also should be listed.

1. Check off the items as they are packed.
2. Keep your packing list handy so you can add to it when you think of additional items.
3. Take the list with you for help in repacking.

ORGANIZING A PACKING
LIST WHEN YOU MOVE

You can cut down on some of the stress of moving by making a list of the contents in each packing container. Place the list at the top of each box before it is closed. Another way is to number each container and number each list. Keep the lists together in a safe place.

ORGANIZING A LIST OF QUESTIONS TO ASK YOUR DOCTOR

Write questions for your doctor as you think of them. Don't wait until just before you leave home to do this. Rank them in order of importance, in case you can't get through them all. One person takes a small notebook with her written questions each time she visits her doctor. She also jots down his answers. This way she has a record of her medical history.

ORGANIZING A LIST OF ISSUES you want to raise at the next club meeting, such as fund raising, organizing a "Senior Strut," or getting a speaker.

ORGANIZING A LIST OF IMPORTANT NUMBERS

Keep this list in your purse or wallet:

- Important phone numbers, such as those of your home, your doctor, a close friend or relative.
- License plate number.
- Social Security number
- Medical insurance number.

ORGANIZING A LIST OF IMPORTANT BIRTHDAYS

A special notebook with the grandchildren's full names and birthdays is a great help. Jotting birthdays down on your monthly calendar keeps you posted.

APPOINTMENT DIARIES AND CALENDARS

Many people rely on appointment diaries and calendars. There is such a variety of them on the market that it's a good idea to experiment to find one that suits you. If a daily, weekly or monthly diary or calendar is going to work most efficiently, it has to meet your needs. Some people are happy with a fairly simple system, while others may need something more elaborate.

The following system combines a portable diary with a large weekly calendar, and seems to be quite effective.

THE ENGAGEMENT DIARY

Keep the engagement diary always with you when you are away from home. Write appointments down immediately. Choose a conventional size, one that is not too heavy, bulky, or too small. The diary will give you only the bare essentials which you will transfer to your weekly calendar regularly.

THE WEEKLY CALENDAR

You can make up a weekly calendar yourself. Make a calendar like the one illustrated on page 83. A fairly large size piece of paper, such as 8½ × 11, is best. When you have made your calendar, which you can do in very short order, transfer any engagements and their times from your diary to the proper day of the week on your calendar. Choose a specific time of the week, perhaps Sunday afternoon or evening, to do this.

In each column you have enough space to jot down everything that has to be done on each day of that week—phone calls, appointments, defrosting food, paying bills, combing the cat, writing to your son, baking cookies for the bazaar, trimming your mous-

Mon. 6/24	Tues. 6/25	Wed. 6/26	Thurs. 6/27	Fri. 6/28	Sat. 6/29	Sun. 6/30
1) Call Leslie	1) Book group-3pm Hanna's	1) Gloria's 9-12:30	1) Vit. C shot 1:30	1) Finlandia pharmacy	1) Clean kitchen cupboard	1) Compost
2) Wash living room window	2) Make newsprint chart	2) Make cookies	2) Sweep basement	2) Lawn chairs	2) Beryl's dinner 6 pm	2) June expenses
3) Work w.m. Gloria, 9-12:30	3) Weed	3) Physio	3) Type	3) Call Norma	3) Sew button on white jacket	3) Call Ottawa
4) Write Maud	4) Call Brook House	4) Fish fertilizer	4) Wash car wax?	4) Bundle newspapers	4) Write Sally	4) Call Eleanor
5) Call Margaret	5) Word processor (friend of M.E.'s)	5) Write Joan		5) Stuff for Salv. Army		5) Letter to advisor
		6) Garden				

tache, etc. Everything you want to remember, important or unimportant, should be put down on your daily list. You can look at the list in the morning and note it all. As you consult the list during the day, you can cross off things you have done (so satisfying!), and add anything else that has occurred to you.

If at the end of the day you haven't finished everything, you might call attention to what is left by circling it or by transferring it to the next day's list. In either case, it is still there before your eyes when you check again.

For this system to work, you must:

—Be *regular* in transferring appointments from your engagement diary to the weekly calendar.

—*Establish a place* for the calendar and always keep it there, along with a pen or pencil, so that you can easily add to it or cancel items. A desk, phone table, or bulletin board are good locations. A bulletin board is ideal since you can use it for posting the calendar along with shopping lists, notices of coming events, and other items that need attention. The important point is that the calendar be always handy and ready to use.

Advantages of this system are:

1. It frees your memory from having to juggle a lot of different and unconnected details.
2. It helps you to organize and manage your time.
3. It helps you to rehearse information by writing it down.
4. It helps you to pay attention to what you want to remember.

Strategy #2:
☞ Be Aware—Cockpit Drills

AVOID WEAR AND TEAR ON THE NERVES

This strategy helps you to concentrate by using the various senses. The word "drill" suggests a self-disciplined routine. That's what it is all about!

CHECKING APPLIANCES BEFORE YOU LEAVE HOME

Check all appliances which should be turned off. To do this, establish a regular routine and stick to it. Begin in the kitchen. As you look at and check each appliance, say aloud, "The stove is off," "The iron is disconnected," "The electric heater is off," "The heating pad is disconnected." Speaking aloud is very important. In this drill you are using your eyes, ears, and voice.

This kind of checking—speaking and using your senses of seeing and hearing—reinforces your attention. The payoff comes when you are downtown and suddenly are stuck with the thought, "Oh my gosh, did I turn off the stove?" You can reply, "Yes," with confidence.

CHECKING CONTENTS OF PURSE OR POCKETS

Before you leave home, check with your eyes and fingers, and say aloud, "I have money . . . bus pass . . . pills, keys, glasses, engagement diary," and so on. Assemble any other things to take with you alongside your purse or coat, and tick them off the same way, using eyes, fingers, ears, and voice.

CHECKING YOUR CAR BEFORE LOCKING
AND LEAVING IT

How to handle two dreaded situations which plague automobile drivers:

1. Locking the keys in the car.
2. Leaving the lights on.

LOCKED CAR DOOR

Every time you park the car, say aloud, "I am taking the keys out of the ignition. I am putting the keys in my purse" (or wherever you always carry your keys). Every time you lock the door check to see that the keys are in the place where they are always kept. If you normally keep the keys in your purse or wallet, don't be satisfied with putting them in your pocket, or holding them in your hand. That won't do. Put them where they belong!

BACKUP PROCEDURE

To ensure greater peace of mind, keep an extra key inside your purse or pocket, just in case you slip on your drill. Or you can get a small magnetic box to hold a spare key and place it under the fender. These boxes are sold in some key shops and in hardware stores.

If your car has a buzzer which warns that your key is still in the ignition, that's a big help. However, not all cars provide that backup warning.

CAR LIGHTS ON

Every time you park your car, *say aloud* as you check the dashboard, "Lights off." Push or turn the headlight button off as you say this.

BACKUP PROCEDURE

Whenever you leave the car, whether it is in bright sunlight, rain, fog, snow, or darkness, make a habit of always glancing at the headlights. Your battery will thank you.

☞ Strategy #3: Be Orderly

A PLACE FOR EVERYTHING

The old saying "A place for everything and everything in its place" does make sense. But for some people orderliness is not always the same as tidiness. They can find order in a very untidy room. However, order, no matter how you look at it, does help to simplify life. Seniors interviewed on the subject have suggested some specific strategies for keeping things under control.

ESTABLISH A SPECIFIC PLACE TO KEEP:

1. glasses when not in use
2. keys
3. dentures
4. medications
5. letters to be answered
6. business mail needing your attention

7. incoming checks
8. bills
9. key to safe deposit box
10. important papers—will, insurance policies, tax notices, etc.

PAYING BILLS

If you pay bills just once a month, establish a place to store them while they are waiting to be paid. Some people find that an accordion file is useful. A cloth shoe bag, the kind that hangs on the back of a door, is also handy. Items to be saved can be stored in each separate compartment: bills in one, letters in another, etc. Make a habit of putting bills in their compartment as soon as they arrive. Set aside a certain day toward the end of the month to pay all your bills. Or use a clipboard. As bills come in, write the name and amount of each bill on a piece of paper and cross them off when the bill is paid. Record the date of payment. Then file the paper and the receipted bills together.

KEEPING TRACK OF PAID BILLS

Fill in the check stub before writing the check. Save the receipted bills and file them in a specific, easy-to-get-at place. Put the receipts in clearly marked envelopes or file folders, allowing one file or envelope for each category such as electric bills, telephone receipts, credit card and department store receipts.

Another way to keep track of your paid bills is to record each check in a book that is sectioned off alphabetically. Under "E," for example, you could record electric bills, check number, amount and the date. In this way, you can see at a glance what you are paying and how your electrical expenses have been running over a period of time.

ROUTINES

Besides having a place for everything, being orderly means setting up and following routines. Some people live by routines. Others feel hemmed in by them, and prefer to "muddle through." Some routines, such as taking required medications, are essential.

REMEMBERING TO TAKE THOSE PILLS

Remembering to take medications as directed by your physician can be a subject of concern. It is very important to set up a system that will be as foolproof as possible. The system can range from simple to elaborate, depending on how many pills you take and how often and when you take them. You will have to experiment to see what works best for you. Some people use something as basic as an egg carton cut to the correct number of compartments to hold a day's medication. Pharmacies sell pill boxes and special compartmentalized containers. But at home, any small container will do. The important thing is to make sure to:

1. Label your daily container with the names of the pills you put in it.
2. Put the container where you will notice it when you need to take your pills.
3. Put the required number of pills in the container each day.

4. Check at the end of each day to see that they have been consumed.
5. If you should forget to take a pill on time, consult your pharmacist or doctor for instructions about what to do.
6. Always store your medication supply in its original container. Take out just enough for each day.

CHORES

Remember the old routines: Monday, washday; Tuesday, ironing; Wednesday . . . and so on. Establishing a regular time for chores, especially the weekly or monthly or occasional ones, helps to remind you to get them done. Again, the calendar can be used as a reminder.

THE TIMER

As well as its use in the kitchen, the stove timer helps to remind you to do other things. Make as full use of it as you can. Here are a few suggestions:

1. Reminder to turn on a specific radio or TV program.
2. Reminder to make a phone call at a certain time.
3. Reminder to leave home at a certain time to have plenty of leeway to catch the bus.

Timers can be bought in hardware stores or in the kitchen section of department stores.

There are many simple strategies to help people register, store and retrieve information as they go about their daily routines. If you have trouble remembering something, it sometimes is a matter of directing enough attention and energy to the problem to figure out an effective way of solving it.

CHAPTER VIII

Other Strategies for Remembering— Using Mnemonic Techniques

Introduction

The name of the Greek Goddess of Memory, Mnemo-
syne, is the source of the word "mnemonics" (pronounced "nimonicks"), which means "the art of
improving or developing the memory." The expression "mnemonic techniques" is sometimes associated
with unusual ways of remembering vast quantities of
information. You may have witnessed the memory
feats of a mnemonist or memory whiz as he thrilled
and mystified his audience with his spectacular ability to remember all kinds of information. A mnemonic
technique in the experience of most of us, however, is

simply a memory aid which we use as we go about our daily lives.

Just as people use diaries, lists and other external reminders, they can train their memory to use internal ones. Internal reminders are generally known as mnemonic techniques.

Originally mnemonic techniques were used when there were no printing presses, and most people did not possess writing materials. Not only did the great orators of Greece and Rome rely on internal memory aids, other people did, too. Because most people could not make lists, keep appointment diaries, calendars, etc., mnemonic skills were very important.

We still use mnemonic techniques on some occasions and they are useful for some kinds of remembering. It is probably worthwhile to master one or two techniques. They can give you additional ways to assist your memory.

SOME EXAMPLES OF MNEMONIC TECHNIQUES FREQUENTLY USED ARE:

1. *Rhyme:* "Thirty days hath September . . ." or "In 14 hundred 92, Columbus sailed the ocean blue" . . . or the children's counting rhyme "One, Two, Buckle My Shoe."

2. *Patterns:* The events of Veterans or Armistice Day are remembered as happening on the 11th hour of the 11th day of the 11th month. Some people look for patterns in their car license plates, telephone numbers, or birth dates.

3. *Acronyms:* NATO is a well-known acronym for anyone who follows world events. It is a word formed by combining the initial letters of the

name North Atlantic Treaty Organization. Other acronyms are NASA, UNESCO.

4. *Sayings:* "Spring forward, fall back" reminds us how to set our clocks ahead for daylight savings time and then back to standard time.
   "Principle is a rule and principal is a pal" helps us to remember the difference in the spelling and meaning of these two words.[15]

Mnemonic techniques are not just tricks. They use principles of registering, retaining and retrieving. However, you need to learn and practice them if they are going to work for you. They rely on your abilities to organize information, make associations, and to visualize. Visualization is basic to learning mnemonic techniques.

USING YOUR IMAGINATION— VISUALIZING AND ASSOCIATING

To visualize is to see pictures in your mind's eye. When imagining, you are visualizing. When you imagine "tree" you see its picture rather than the word t-r-e-e. It is easier to see concrete pictures in your mind's eye than to see abstract ones. For example, you see an orange more easily than a fruit, or you picture a stabbing more easily than a crime.

Often when you register a picture image, you register words with it. When this happens, you file information both visually and verbally. Or when you register a picture you may also imagine the other senses. For instance, as you imagine a cat in your lap you can also imagine hearing its purr, touching its fur and smelling its clean faint odor. Visualization is not strictly confined to seeing only with the mind's eye.

MAKE YOUR PICTURE COME ALIVE

To be useful, visualization must be vivid. When you use other senses they help your imaginative picture come alive. To practice visualization pick something concrete. Surround it with details so that you can practically touch, feel, smell and taste it. If you wish to visualize a lemon meringue pie, for instance, see its bright yellow filling and fluffy white meringue, smell its piquant aroma, feel the crusty meringue, taste the lemon flavor.

Another way to produce vivid images is to exaggerate them, make them ridiculous, or include some action. The more unusual the image, the easier it is to remember. For example, "pills" might be imagined as large capsules a foot long, with mixed colors in stripes lined up one against another in a bathtub.

✔ PRACTICE VISUALIZATION

Make the following items into vivid images and describe them:

ITEMS	DESCRIPTION OF VIVID IMAGE
Bread	
Umbrella	
Dinner	
Doctor's Appointment	

The left side of the brain is often said to deal more with logic, reasoning and language; the right side of the brain more with imagination, images, and the senses. In school we were often rewarded for using the "left side" of the brain. Visualization relies heavily on the "right side"—seeing with the mind's eye and exercising the imagination.

Learning to think in pictures can take time and may seem artificial to those who rarely do it. However, visualization is very rewarding when you see that it really does help you to remember.

All mnemonic techniques depend on visualization and on associations—connecting what you are trying to remember with what is already familiar to you. The mnemonic techniques known as the Method of Loci, Peg Word System, and Name Recall are all based on association. When you use these techniques you are using visualization to help form associations.

Method of Loci

One of the oldest ways of aiding recall is the Method of Loci. (It means method of locations and is pronounced "low kye.") This mnemonic technique dates back to ancient Greece and Rome. It is based on the idea that people remember familiar locations easily and use the locations as clues to recall information associated with them. It consists of two steps:

1. Link something to be remembered with a specific place.
2. To recall the item, just remember the location.

The system is basically simple. You start with a place you know well, such as your home. Visualize a series of locations within your home in a consistent order. An easy way to do this is to start at the front door (location 1), enter the living room (location 2), go from there to the dining room (location 3), into the kitchen (location 4), and on to the bedrooms, the bathroom and so on. If you should need more clues to help you recall, you can subdivide the space in a particular room. For example, within the kitchen you might visualize the refrigerator as a location, the stove as another, the eating area as another. See these familiar locations clearly and distinctly in your mind's eye. Make sure that you have established a set of locations that you always see in the same order.

"In the first place . . ."

The next step is to associate the new information, in the order you wish it to be remembered, with a particular location in the house.

For example, suppose you want to remember a number of errands you have to do. You intend to make a deposit at the bank and go to the community center for this month's birthday celebrations. Then you will stop at the post office to get stamps and to mail letters. Afterwards you will go to the drugstore to buy vitamin C.

If you associate going to the bank with your *front door* you might visualize deposit slips stuck all over your door. As you enter the *living room*, you might see a giant red, white, and blue birthday cake which says "Happy Birthday March Members." In the *dining room*, three letters on the table have big flags standing on each of them saying, "mail me." Going into the *kitchen*, you have to be careful because there are stamps stuck everywhere—on the fridge door, the counters, the stove, and your fingers stick to them. In the *bedroom* the dresser is overflowing with purple vitamin C tablets.

For this system to work it is essential that you visualize vividly your locations and the items you want to connect with them. Form strong clear associations between each location and each item.

✔ USING THE METHOD OF LOCI

1. Write a list of items to remember.
2. Sketch the layout of your home.
3. In your mind's eye see the first item on your list at your front door, the second in your living room, etc.
4. Now write down the list from memory.

The Method of Loci can be used for remembering items on shopping lists, things to do, names, speeches, and so on. It can also be used to help file a thought which comes into your head. You can pin it down by visualizing it in a specific location in your home, say, in the dining room or kitchen. Hours or even days later, when you are wondering what you were thinking about, you can imagine the location and your thought will reappear if you have not used the method again in the meantime.

Peg Word System

The Peg Word System is very effective and can produce dramatic results. It is probably the most famous technique used by memory dazzlers, entertainers, and serious students of memory training.

1, 2 Buckle my shoe.
  3, 4 Shut the door.
5, 6 Pick up sticks.
  7, 8 Lay them straight.
9, 10 A big fat hen.

The Peg Word System is so named because it provides "pegs" on which to hang unrelated words or ideas you wish to remember. The peg words do two things:

1. They help you to organize the material you wish to remember.
2. They also act as reminders to recall that material.

LEARNING THE PEG WORDS

Memorize the following ten concrete, easily visualized words that rhyme with the numbers one through ten. Read them aloud.

1. One is a bun
2. Two is a shoe
3. Three is a tree
4. Four is a door
5. Five is a hive
6. Six are sticks
7. Seven is heaven
8. Eight is a gate
9. Nine is a vine
10. Ten is a hen

You doubtless have noticed the similarity of the peg words to the nursery rhyme "One, Two, Buckle My Shoe." You can probably learn quickly which words represent which numbers.

DRAW YOUR PEG WORD PICTURES

Visualize the object which each peg word represents. Now draw a picture of a bun, a shoe, a tree, etc. The results of your artwork may cause a chuckle, but the very act of drawing the pictures helps to fix the rhyming words in your memory.

Once you have a strong association between the numbers and the words that rhyme with them, you have constructed your pegs. Test yourself. See each peg word picture as you say it aloud: Bun— Shoe— Tree— Door— Hive— Sticks— Heaven— Gate— Vine— Hen—. Now skip around and see the peg words for 6, 3, 8, 1, 4, 10, 7, 9, 2, 5. You will notice that the peg word method provides you with flexibility. You don't have to depend on the order 1–10 to keep you on track.

HOW TO USE THE PEG WORD SYSTEM

Using the Peg Word System you can easily remember many items. You attach the words or ideas you want to remember to the pegs.

Suppose you wish to remember to buy ten items: carrots, Kleenex, cat food, milk, ginger ale, a prescription drug, stamps, ballpoint pen, nails, and birdseed.

Attach each separate item from your list to one of the peg word pictures in your mind. When you do this, try to make the picture of the paired items as vivid as possible. Cast aside literal pictures and have some fun. The effectiveness of these word pairs relies on slightly ridiculous sets of mental pictures, depending on exaggeration.

You might visualize the first item as a six-foot-high bright orange *carrot* balanced on a bun(1). For *Kleenex*, you might see your shoe (2) stuffed with so much green Kleenex that it is overflowing. For *cat food* a tree (3) may be loaded with cans of cat food hanging from its branches, weighing them down. You might have a carton of *milk* balanced precariously on the top of your door (4). *Ginger ale* bottles with bees swarming around them might surround a hive (5). For the sixth item, a huge *prescription* pill bottle might be covered by a pile of sticks (6). You might see a stairway made of *stamps* in a long unbroken line reaching up to heaven (7). For the eighth item, you might see *ball-point pens* made into a gate (8). Your ninth picture might include a huge *nail* with a vine (9) twisting around it. You might see a hen (10) carrying a *box of birdseed* under her wing for your tenth picture. When you think "bun" you see the carrot; when you think "shoe" you see Kleenex, and so on. The peg words organize and provide clues that catch your mind's eye and hold your interest.

Any image that is slightly silly or absurd both adds to the enjoyment and helps you to recall what it is you wish to remember.

Your peg words can be used over and over again for different lists. As soon as you make new associations with the pegs, the previous associations are wiped out. Once you are finished with one list, the pegs are cleared, ready to use with another list.

The peg word method provides you with a stable, efficient file system for keeping information in your head. Each peg is a clue to recalling the item associated with it. All you have to do is go to the peg to find it. You can recall items in order from one through ten, or just as easily in a random order within the numbers 1–10. For people who wish to expand their peg words beyond ten, there is an enlarged system of peg words which can be found in the following popular books on memory.

Furst, Bruno. *Stop Forgetting*. Garden City; Doubleday
and Co., 1979.
Higbee, Kenneth L. *Your Memory, How It Works and
How to Improve It*. Englewood Cliffs; Prentice-Hall,
1977.
Lorayne, Harry, and Jerry Lucas. *The Memory Book*.
New York; Stein & Day, 1974.

WHEN TO USE THE PEG WORD SYSTEM

Peg words are useful in remembering shopping lists,
errands and other things to be done. They can also help
you to organize the various activities of your day by
letting you know just where you are in a series of
tasks that you have planned. The peg word system can
give you a feeling of being in control. However, like
any mnemonic technique, it has to be mastered. Still
it can be fun to do.

✔ PRACTICE USING THE PEG WORD SYSTEM

Make Your Own Shopping List:

1.	6.
2.	7.
3.	8.
4.	9.
5.	10.

✔ VISUALIZE YOUR ITEMS CONNECTED
WITH THE PEG WORDS. DESCRIBE
THESE PICTURES BELOW.

1.   6.

2.   7.

3.   8.

4.   9.

5.   10.

See if you can recall the items to be remembered in order, out of order, and even backwards. You might try to repeat this exercise with other lists.

What's in a Name—
Remembering
Names and Faces

Your name represents your roots and your individuality. It represents who you are. When you go some place, perhaps into a store or restaurant, or to church, or the senior center, and are greeted by name, you feel that you are someone special, and not just anyone. By remembering a person's name you indirectly give that person a message that he or she is unique. In effect, you are saying, "I recognize that you are you and not just anybody." Because people's names are so important, many of us get embarrassed when we find we cannot remember them.

SOME REASONS WHY WE CAN'T REMEMBER NAMES

- We don't pay attention or rehearse the name enough to register it.

- We may get more easily distracted with increasing age.
- We are tense or preoccupied.
- We are thinking of another name when we mean to say the correct name.

Remembering faces seems to give less trouble than remembering names. When someone says "I know your face but I can't remember your name" it is because:

- It is generally easier to remember things you see than those you hear.
- Recognition is easier than recall. Identifying a face involves recognition; remembering a name involves recall.

To help you remember names and faces,
try these four steps:

—Make sure you register the person's name.
—Associate the name with something
meaningful and concrete.
—Note the distinctive features of the person's face.
—Form a visual association between the name
and the distinctive features of the face.

MAKE SURE YOU REGISTER THE NAME

When you are introduced to someone, you generally hear his or her name only once. It may be a strange-sounding name, spoken quickly, softly, or glossed over. You may be noticing other people in the room at the same time, concerned about the impression you are making, or eager to meet someone else. All of these reasons, plus many others, can easily distract you and keep you from registering the name.

Even if you have heard the name correctly, the entire introduction might have taken less than two or three seconds. Hearing the name only once is usually not enough for it to register. To register a name adequately you have to rehearse it by repeating it several times. You might try to use the name in conversation, or perhaps to spell it or ask the person to spell it. If you can repeat it or hear it repeated three or four times, you will probably remember it. Paying attention—concentrating on the person and his or her name—is essential.

ASSOCIATE THE NAME WITH SOMETHING MEANINGFUL AND CONCRETE

Some concrete names, such as Lyons, Bird, Fox, Woods, Underhill, Carpenter, Taylor, are all fairly easy to imagine. Difficulties in visualizing arise when the name you are trying to remember is neither meaningful nor concrete. To get around this you can break up the syllables of the name into smaller words that have similar sounds and will also give you a concrete image. For example, the name "Begalsporz" could be broken into the words "beagle's paws," and you might see a beagle licking its paws.

In *The Memory Book*, Lorayne and Lucas have compiled a list of names and suggested substitute words to help visualize them. The following names and substitute words are part of that list.

Anderson—hand-and-son
Dougherty—dough-or-tea, or dock-her-tea
Harrison—hairy son
Morris—more-rice
Udall—you-doll[15]

✔ MAKE UP YOUR OWN SUBSTITUTE WORDS

NAME	WORD SUBSTITUTES
Parkinson	
Hammerman	
Gose	
O'Hara	

NOTE THE DISTINCTIVE FEATURES OF THE FACE

To form a strong link between the name and the face you want to remember you need to make a vivid and concrete association. If you are not used to looking closely at a person's face, you may have difficulty finding something distinctive in it. However, some faces are more memorable than others. Very attractive or unattractive faces are generally easy to register. Faces belonging to your own race are easier to remember than those of other races. You can train yourself to find one or two distinguishing characteristics that stand out in a particular face, such as a person's eyes, or smile, or chin.

FORM A VISUAL ASSOCIATION BETWEEN THE NAME AND THE DISTINCTIVE FEATURES OF THE FACE

Suppose you have just met Mrs. Jones. She has a round face with broad cheekbones. First register her name and make it meaningful. You could do this by substituting the word "bones" for Jones, and picturing bones in your mind's eye. As you look carefully at her face you might decide that her broad cheeks are her most distinguishing feature. Find a way of linking the name and the outstanding features in a vivid and concrete way. Perhaps you might see large soup bones jammed into each enormously puffed-out cheek. Whenever you see Mrs. Jones, you will see her cheeks, be reminded of bones in her cheeks and the bones will give you the clue for her name.

In the old joke, when Mrs. Smith was trying to remember Mr. Kelly's name she noticed that he had a large paunch, so she paired Kelly with "belly." The following day when she saw Mr. Kelly she greeted him with "How do you do, Mr. Stomach." There *is* the danger that you may forget the original name for which you have used meaningful substitute words!

To Remember Someone's Name

1. Listen and hear the name. Repeat it.
2. Give the name meaning.
3. Look attentively at the face. Notice one or more outstanding features.
4. Link the meaningful name and the distinguishing feature(s) in a vivid, dramatic picture in your mind's eye.

These four steps are generally used in everyday situations, sometimes consciously and sometimes automatically. If you practice them, your ability to remember names and faces will improve significantly.

✔ PRACTICE NAME RECALL

Write the names of five people whom you know and identify their outstanding features. Associate their names and features.

Over the next two weeks, do the same exercise with names of people you have recently met. Practice with a friend.

Mnemonic Techniques—
Summary

The Method of Loci, the Peg Word System and Name Recall all have a playful quality about them in their use of imagination, humor and exaggeration. It is this which make them helpful as mnemonic techniques because they make use of your wit to strengthen your ability to remember. Although mnemonic techniques may have limited practicality, they can be very effective in helping you to register, retain and retrieve specific pieces of information.

Mnemonic techniques sharpen your wits.

CHAPTER IX

Lifestyle and Memory— Putting It All Together

Body—Mind—Spirit

"Each of us is . . . [composed] of a body, mind and spirit. These . . . are so closely interwoven that it is impossible to draw a boundary line between them. What affects one, affects all, and each . . . affects the other."[16]

It is not possible to talk about memory changes in aging without also recognizing the close connection of our memory with our bodies, minds, feelings, and spirits. All are interrelated and work together to make us who we are. Our memories affect and are affected by the state of our whole being.

We know that on our "good days" we feel at peace with our bodies, our minds are clear and alert, and our outlook is positive. We feel integrated, and we realize that our minds, bodies, and emotions are all working together in harmony.

On the other hand, "bad days" caused by stress, fatigue, depression or illness are unsatisfying and unpleasant. Our bodies and emotions are uncomfortable and sometimes painful, our minds preoccupied and disturbed by negative thoughts. We feel off balance and out of touch with ourselves. If we stop to observe, we clearly realize that body, mind and spirit are each influencing one another. Their integration is essential to regain a feeling of balance and wholeness. When one of the parts is in need, the resources of the others must be called upon to help. Nowhere is this better illustrated than when there are changes in a person's body.

Here is an account of one man's awareness of himself as a whole human being:

Thanks to enlightened modern hospital practice I was able to go home 48 hours after a hernia operation. But since I am an older person, I also attribute my quick recovery to more personal qualities. My body is in good condition from regular daily exercise. I watch my diet carefully— lots of fruits and vegetables, vitamin supplements, no red meat, little alcohol, and no smoking. I was in a ward, which meant I had to respond to others rather than withdraw into my pain and worries. I talked frequently with a cheerful young man in the bed opposite me and did not get too involved with my other roommate whose negative thinking appeared to be slowing down his recovery. Since I wanted to go home as soon as possible, I did what I could to help myself by drinking a

lot of fluids and taking short walks. On one round of the corridors, I was whistling. A passing nurse smiled and said, "That's a nice sound." We both felt good. I followed as much of my usual daily routine as possible, especially my meditation and prayers before starting each day.

After I returned home I continued to recuperate well. But I began to take on more of my usual responsibilities before I had completely recovered. I felt bothered by things that normally would not bother me. I felt tense and noticed that I tended to be forgetful and not as sharp as usual. Eventually, with more time and healing, I regained my ability to handle the challenges and problems of my life in a more balanced and realistic way.

The holistic view of life helps us to appreciate all aspects of ourselves, including memory. Instead of associating memory exclusively with the working of the brain, as most "memory improvement" books do, we realize that bodily and mental states, emotional and inner spiritual resources, all influence the way memory works.

With this in mind, we shall take a brief look at various parts of our lifestyles which have some bearing on the ability to remember. The body and mind are strongly influenced by what we eat and drink, and by medications, smoking, stress, physical activity and relaxation. All of these also affect the memory. The mind, emotions and spirit are connected with feelings of self-worth. Memory is influenced by how we feel about ourselves. Body, mind and spirit are all involved in the journey to self-acceptance and the attainment of wisdom. Memory plays an important part in this journey.

An understanding of how
memory works is incomplete
without some acknowledgment
of the whole human being.

How Does Nutrition
Affect Your Memory?

Eating is very important to most people, and what we eat affects our well-being to a profound degree. Not only are our bodies and minds nourished by what we consume, our feelings are influenced as well. We can feel loved and loving as we eat or prepare a special dish that is dear to our hearts and stomachs. We associate eating certain foods with important occasions, such as Thanksgiving and Christmas dinner, Passover and Easter feasts, birthdays and anniversaries. Food is a part of many important customs and rituals in our lives. On these occasions it means much more than simply fuel for the body.

On a daily basis, what we eat is even more essential to the relationship of our bodies, minds and feelings. The well-being that comes from eating what our bodies actually require affects the alertness of our minds and our outlook on life.

Food influences how the brain works and has a significant effect on its functioning. Some older people living alone can't be bothered "cooking for one," and may resort to tea and toast or other kinds of inadequate and unbalanced diets. When this happens their bodies suffer and are unable to serve them well. Eventually these people begin to experience memory difficulties.

Although scientists do not know precisely how nutrition affects memory, they do know that certain imbalances in the diet do cause problems. They know that children's ability to remember is affected by iron deficiency, food additives, too much sugar and too little protein. These lead to short attention span, fidgeting and irritability. Imbalances in certain vitamins and minerals also appear to play a part in problems with memory. Some researchers maintain that what applies to children applies to adults as well.

People are used to eating certain kinds and quantities of food when they are physically active. As they become less active they may find it difficult to change their eating habits. As bodies age and the metabolism rate slows they need fewer calories. Although people may eat less, their bodies, including their brains, still need the same amount of vitamins and minerals. They need to maintain a varied, balanced diet, but one with fewer calories.

Older people cannot afford to eat empty calories such as sugar, which has very poor nutritional value and is implicated in a number of diseases. Nor can they afford to eat junk food which is loaded with sugar, fat, salt and food additives.

Slowing down of the waste disposal system often results in constipation. Since constipation can lead to mental sluggishness and irritability, it has an effect on memory. Increased roughage or fiber, such as bran and other whole grains, can help considerably to overcome this problem.

As people age, their sense of thirst is reduced. It is easy to forget to drink an adequate amount of water every day. Yet it is very important that older people drink a minimum of six to eight glasses of fluids a day.

Water assists in:
• Combatting constipation
• Absorbing medications
• Improving digestion
• Good kidney functioning
• Mental alertness

Dehydration is common among older people. Lack of water in the body has a direct and profound effect on memory. Dehydration leads to difficulties in thinking and to confusion.

Much has been written about the importance in the diet of vitamins A and D, B, C, and E, and such minerals as calcium, magnesium, iron, zinc, and others. Although there is still controversy about the benefits of taking vitamin and mineral supplements, many older people feel that supplements enhance their vigor and well-being. Medical scientists do not agree on how many vitamin and mineral supplements are needed in the diets of older people and in what quantities. Read as much as you can about recent discoveries and check the trustworthiness of the authority you are reading. You will have to come to your own conclusions about vitamin and mineral supplements. The jury is still out on the issue.

According to most nutritionists, the majority of adults in North America should drastically reduce sugar, fats, and salt in their diets. They should significantly increase the quantity and variety of vegetables, fruits and whole grains they eat. They should eat moderate amounts of protein, such as meats, poultry, eggs, and dairy products.

THE SENSE OF WELL-BEING IS AFFECTED BY:

—Quality of food eaten.
—Quantity of food eaten.
—Variety of food eaten.
—Amount of fluids drunk.
—Kinds and quantity of vitamins and minerals consumed.
—Consumption of salt, sugar, fat, food additives.

When people eat the right amount of a good variety of nutritious food and drink adequate amounts of water each day, when they get enough vitamins and minerals, when they cut down on salt, sugar, fat and food additives—they are treating their bodies right. One of the payoffs is that they are also helping their memory to be more efficient.

Memory and Recreational Drugs—Alcohol, Tobacco, Coffee and Tea

"Alcohol and aging, working together, may cause more damage to brain cells than either one would cause by itself." (*Prevention*, June 1984)

The quotation from *Prevention* magazine may be rather distressing to older people whose way of life includes drinking alcohol. Many people consider that social drinking enhances their lives. They associate it with relaxing in pleasant company and with good times. However, problems arise when social drinking turns into habitual drinking which makes a person dependent on alcohol. No matter what his or her age, this puts wear and tear on the drinker's body, including the brain. But an older adult who is a habitual drinker will probably experience even greater damage than a younger person will.

The *Alcoholism and Aging* publication of SPARC states, "The effects of alcohol depend on the age, mood, and health of the drinker. . . . If you are over 55 you may be drinking the same amount as you always have, but the effects are different. . . . The amount of alcohol in the body builds up [more quickly] and the effects remain longer."[17]

Alcohol is quickly absorbed into the bloodstream, and there are no barriers preventing it from passing directly to the brain. This process can take as short a time as five minutes. It takes only a .08 alcohol level in the blood for a person to experience a state of euphoria and to have his or her judgment clouded.

ALCOHOLIC IMPAIRMENT OF MEMORY

An older person requires less alcohol than a younger one to become addicted to drinking. Even two or three drinks about four or five times a week on a regular basis will lower the ability to remember, and the more someone drinks the more his or her memory can be impaired. A drinker often has trouble remembering things that happen while he is intoxicated. The most extreme case of non-recall is alcoholic black-out.

The amount of alcohol consumed at any one time also affects the ability to remember. It has been discovered that alcohol seems to affect women's ability to remember more than it does men's. Women appear to absorb and eliminate alcohol more slowly, and tend to get "higher" than men do on the same amount of alcohol.[18]

ALCOHOL AND MEDICATIONS

Many older people take medication on a regular basis. Alcohol can be particularly harmful when taken together with a number of different medications. Alcohol should NEVER be taken along with barbiturates, blood pressure pills, heart pills, antibiotics, and tranquilizers. The combination of certain drugs and alcohol can multiply the effect of the drug as much as tenfold. This can result in confusion, drowsiness, deep sleep, and, at the most extreme, even coma.

TOBACCO, COFFEE, AND TEA

Along with alcohol, tobacco, coffee, and tea are also considered to be recreational drugs. People dependent on smoking and drinking large amounts of coffee and tea are actually taking recreational drugs which affect the memory.

TOBACCO

Smoking cuts down the amount of oxygen that gets to the brain. Lowered oxygen levels result in decreased memory efficiency. Researchers have found that smokers consistently score lower than non-smokers on memory tests.

COFFEE AND TEA

The stimulating effect of caffeine is the reason why so many people feel they need a cup of coffee or tea to start the day. Being stimulated generally helps in the registering stage of memory. However, in large amounts, caffeine causes irritability, which affects concentration and contributes to distractibility. Too much caffeine can actually cause problems in registering. Because it often disturbs sleep, caffeine can also lead to fatigue and fuzzy-mindedness.

It takes approximately four hours for caffeine to go through the body, and more than three cups a day can contribute to over-irritability, high blood pressure, and ulcers. Tea contains less caffeine than coffee, but the tannic acid in tea can be even more stimulating.

All recreational drugs—alcohol, tobacco, coffee, tea— should be taken in moderation. Although we can't always see the immediate effects of smoking, and of drinking tea and coffee, they should be used with the knowledge that they are not harmless.

Medications and Memory

The lifestyle of many older people includes taking medication. The correct medication in the correct dosage can add considerably to the quality of life, improving physical well-being, mood, and clarity of thought. But sometimes there is a price to pay for taking medication. Part of the price is the effects that some drugs can have on memory.

Although their main purpose is to treat specific problems, drugs also produce side effects on other parts of the body. Some drugs also interact with other drugs. While main and side effects of a pill are usually known and predictable, the interaction of two or more pills can cause unpleasant or unhealthy reactions which are often unpredictable. Side effects and drug interactions can have a significant impact on an individual's personality and mental functioning.

All medications have a number of effects on the body, and all drugs have some limitations. The key is to weigh the benefits of taking a drug against its negative effects and make a calculated choice about whether the benefits outweigh the disadvantages. This kind of decision should be made in consultation with your doctor.

Many drugs affect mood, alertness, and ability to deal with new information. Medications such as sleeping pills, tranquilizers, muscle relaxants, and anti-anxiety drugs sometimes produce confusion and memory loss. There are also a number of drugs which cause depression as a side effect.

Any medication labeled with the precaution "Don't drive" will probably also impair your ability to remember. Over-the-counter drugs, such as cold tablets or allergy tablets which contain antihistamines, produce drowsiness and also affect the ability to remember. The following drugs can hinder vision, alertness, judgment, and ability to concentrate:

—alcohol
—tranquilizers

—painkillers that contain narcotics
—motion sickness pills
—barbiturates

Today's medications, including non-prescription drugs, are very potent and complex. It is a good idea to develop a healthy respect for any drug you take. If you are having memory problems, check with your doctor and/or pharmacist to see if your difficulty could be partly a result of the medications you are taking. It is very important that main effects, side effects, and drug interactions be carefully monitored. Since everyone reacts to drugs somewhat differently, note carefully how drugs affect you.

Handling Stress and Tension

Stress and tension are a part of daily life. You feel them in your body, mind and spirit. Actually, some stress is caused by positive events, but what most people feel as tension comes from troubles and problems. Although most older adults have an extraordinary ability to adapt to change, some life events can cause a great deal of stress. Stress affects mood and mood affects the ability to remember.

Small incidents, many having to do with forgetting, can also produce stress and tension. For example, suppose you have an appointment at ten o'clock. It is now 9:50, you can't find the house keys and you are flustered. Or you go to a store to buy a book. The title and author are on the tip of your tongue but you can't recall them and you feel foolish. Or you've forgotten your umbrella on the bus and you are annoyed with yourself. This kind of experience can produce a knot in your stomach, sweaty palms, tensed muscles, trembling, and sometimes even a pounding heart or a headache.

These physical sensations interfere with your ability to concentrate. They do not let you ramble through your memory storage files to recall the information you need. You try harder and harder to remember, but go blank. The stress of forcing yourself to remember blocks the remembering process. Many people seek release from this kind of tension by smoking, drinking alcohol, increased medication, and increased or decreased eating or sleeping.

DECREASING TENSION

Tension needs to be kept within reasonable limits. Decreasing tension can often be accomplished by talking over problems with someone who is close to you, taking a break from the tension-producing situation, exercising regularly, and learning how to relax. A positive side effect of decreasing tension is that you often will be able to remember something you have forgotten.

Relaxing is easier said than done, especially when you have perfectly good cause to be nervous and tense. Specific relaxation techniques can help, but they all require learning and regular practice. However, people who are willing to practice find them very beneficial.

Learning to breathe deeply, slowly and evenly is particularly important in achieving a state of relaxed well-being. Among the proven techniques that will help you to relax are yoga and tai-chi, with their emphasis on slow meditative movements and on relaxing deep breathing. Along with meditation, these disciplines help to calm both the body and the mind.

Swimming and walking are excellent ways of helping yourself to relax. Progressive relaxation is also an effective technique. It is a step-by-step method for relieving tension by tensing and relaxing muscle groups throughout your body.

Some people benefit from the technique of assertiveness training. This training teaches how to give and receive information clearly and how to claim your rights in a tactful, straightforward manner. These skills help to reduce or avoid tension in many situations.

Above all, an irrepressible sense of humor adds zest to life and offers marvelous instant relief from many stressful moments.

There are other techniques to reduce stress. You can find courses in relaxation offered in such places as community centers, the YWCA, YMCA, senior centers, community colleges, and universities.

The following books on stress management have been found to be helpful.

Geba, Bruno. *Breathe Away Your Tension.* New York; Random House/Bookworks, 1973.

Huang, Al Chun-liang. *Embrace Tiger, Return to Mountain: The Essence of Tai Chi.* Moab, Utah; Real People Press, 1973.

Jacobson, Edmond. *Progressive Relaxation.* Chicago; University of Chicago Press, 1971.

Mitchell, Laura. *Simple Relaxation—The Physiological Method for Easing Tension.* London; John Murray Publishers, 1977.

Nuernberger, Phil. *Freedom from Stress—A Holistic Approach.* Honesdale, Pa.; Himalayan International Institute of Yoga Science and Philosophy Publishers, 1981.

Physical Activity
and Memory

The once popular idea that people become too old to exercise is no longer accepted. We now know that physical activity is necessary for an older person's health and sense of well-being. Many studies show that people over fifty need more physical activity. Exercise is essential to all parts of the body, including the brain. An exercise program for people in their sixties and seventies showed that participants improved their muscle strength, increased the density of their bones, significantly increased their oxygen intake, and reduced their blood pressure. These last two benefits both have positive effects on the functioning of the brain.

Most mild exercises for older people, including those who are physically handicapped, attempt to improve the flexibility of joints and increase the capacity of the heart and lungs. The stimulation of the heart and lungs increases the amount of oxygen carried through the bloodstream to the brain. Lack of exercise not only makes you physically sluggish, it makes you mentally sluggish as well. People who exercise regularly or are generally physically active remember more quickly and are also able to improve their speed of recall.

A reasonable level of energy is necessary for using your memory efficiently. To build up energy levels you must first exercise. You can start with very small amounts every day and gradually increase the demands on your body. This will increase your fitness. But fitness cannot be stored. To maintain it you must keep exercising regularly several times a week. Approximately twenty minutes per day, three times a week, seems to be a minimum amount of exercise time needed to produce any beneficial impact on your body. Brisk walking, swimming, yoga, gardening and dancing are all excellent forms of exercise.

POSTURE

The brain needs far more blood, and the oxygen it carries, than other body organs do. Poor posture constricts the arteries to the brain and cuts down on the amount of blood that flows into it. Slouching produces rounded shoulders and jutting chin. It throws the upper body out of alignment, creates stress and strain, and contributes to unclear thinking and forgetfulness. Good posture, important throughout life, remains so as people age. But poor posture is a habit which is hard to break.

Simply exercising your body will not do much to correct posture. However, techniques such as yoga and tai-chi, both particularly suited to older people, can be useful. With their emphasis on body awareness, breathing, relaxation, and concentration on each aspect of movement, they can help you to pay more attention to your posture by becoming more aware of your whole body.

SOME OF THE BENEFITS FROM REGULAR PHYSICAL ACTIVITY

Enjoyable physical activity makes you feel good. It lightens your heart and clears your head as it stimulates circulation and limbers you up. No matter what a person's physical limitations are, physical activity is a must for health of body and mind. It is often recommended to people who are feeling sad or depressed. Some researchers believe that it is impossible to be both depressed and physically active at the same time. The body manufactures certain chemicals during activity which tend to produce a mood-lifting effect on the mind.

Physical activity also helps to reduce tension, and this can change your way of dealing with the world. A heightened sense of well-being, better sleep, ability to accomplish tasks with greater ease, and improved relationships with friends and family are often some of the outcomes of regular exercise.

Exercise affects memory directly through stimulating the blood supply to the brain. It also contributes to a better memory as it contributes to good health in general. One memory expert claims, "When you feel good, look good, and are bounding with energy, your mind can process information faster and better, and remembering is easier."[19]

EXERCISE BENEFITS MEMORY BY INCREASING:

1. Mental alertness
2. Energy levels
3. Sense of well-being
4. Relaxation

The following materials on exercise have been found to be helpful.

Take It Easy But Take It! An Exercise Program for the Older Canadian. Government of Canada Fitness and Amateur Sport, 1980. [free]

Fun and Fitness 1 Instructor's Manual. The Canadian Red Cross Society, 1979.

Christensen, Alice, and David Rankin. *Easy Does It Yoga for Older People*. San Francisco; Harper and Row, 1975.

Frankel, Lawrence J., and Betty Byrd Richard. *Be Alive as Long as You Live—The Older Person's Complete Guide to Exercise for Joyful Living*. New York; Lippincott and Crowell, 1980.

Luce, Gay Gaer. *Your Second Life—Vitality and Growth in Middle and Later Years*. New York; Delacorte Press/Seymour Lawrence, 1979.

Young, Beryl, and Kathleen Gose. *Reach for the Sun! Chair Exercises for Elderly People*. (cassette tape and manual) Vancouver; Joy of Fitness Production Company c/o B.C. Health Association, 1982.

Self-Worth and Memory

How you feel about yourself influences the way you think and behave. When you feel generally secure about yourself you are able to acknowledge your own worth, accepting your weaknesses along with your strengths and appreciating yourself for who you are. Your sense of self-worth controls your outlook on life. It also affects your memory, both directly and indirectly.

If you have gone through some difficult times, and have found that you cannot think clearly, have found it hard to concentrate or retain what you have heard or read, check your feelings of self-worth.

Ask yourself:

1. What am I doing with my time?
2. Am I doing things that make me feel as if I am achieving something or making a contribution to someone?

3. Have I put any energy into contacting friends or acquaintances to maintain these relationships?
4. Do I have someone with whom I feel safe and can unburden myself and just be me?

As people grow older their sense of self-worth often needs to be nurtured. They need to remember to be good to themselves, to value and acknowledge their inner beauty, the spirit within. Some sources which help to increase a sense of self-worth are:

—Work or other meaningful activity
—Friends and other social contacts
—Intimate relationships

Work is any activity which allows you the opportunity to contribute, to feel useful, and to achieve. It may include anything from paid work, volunteering, helping family and friends, to working on developing your own personal interests. Contributing to yourself, your family, friends or community is a great morale booster.

As people age their world often changes, and it becomes increasingly important to reach out, to nurture and develop a circle of friends and acquaintances. Everyone needs to bask in the warmth and light that come from friends. Sometimes friends become a life support when it is needed most. With retirement there is more time and energy to cultivate new and old friendships. Social contacts from clubs, church and neighborhood also help to increase the pleasure in living.

Many people think that the term "intimate relationships" refers only to a husband and wife or to two lovers. An intimate relationship can be formed with anyone who becomes a close confidant and is an important person in your life. He or she might be a son or daughter, or a dear friend. Some people may even find an intimate relationship with a pet which accepts them and never lets them down. There is increasing evidence of the importance of pets in the health and well-being of older adults.

SELF-WORTH FINALLY COMES FROM WITHIN

There is no magic formula for building a strong sense of self-worth. Each person finds it in his or her own way. But people who are active and contributing to others are also contributing to themselves. Some people do this by devoting most of their time to work or other meaningful activities. Others maintain their self-worth in the company of friends and acquaintances, as part of a group where they feel they "belong." Still others feel a sense of fulfillment as part of a couple. They are happy and content to spend their time almost exclusively with a loving spouse. The sense of self-worth can come from many sources or combination of circumstances. However, it finally comes from within—from the belief that "I am a valuable person, not only in the eyes of other people but in my own eyes as well."

"I am a valuable person not only in the eyes of other people but in my own eyes as well."

It is a good idea to be aware of the people and the circumstances which help you to appreciate yourself, and to cultivate them. Increased feelings of self-worth also increase the ability to think clearly and to remember. A life that contains meaningful activity and relationships provides energy, zest and interest—all things that help your memory to work for you.

The Ulyssean Adult—Creativity in the Middle and Later Years, by John A. B. McLeish, is an excellent book by an older adult on the subject of self-worth in later life.

Lifestyle and Memory— Summary

A variety of influences affect each person's lifestyle. These influences also affect the ability to be clear-headed and alert.

—The quality and quantity of what we eat, and what we drink
—The medications we take
—The physical activity we regularly do
—The amount of stress in our lives and how we handle it
—Our feelings of self-worth, stemming from satisfaction with the quality of our lives.

All of these influence the ability to remember. Although each one has been dealt with separately, they don't belong in pigeon holes, isolated from one another. Each is connected in its own way with all the others.

How we take care of our bodies affects our minds and emotions. How we feel about ourselves affects the health of our bodies, minds and emotions. Changing any one part of what makes up a lifestyle brings changes in the other parts. Our personal lifestyles reflect attitudes we have about ourselves—our values and our beliefs as they demonstrate who we are and what we do.

Our personal lifestyles reflect our attitudes, our values, and our beliefs.

Our attention in this chapter has been primarily on body, mind and emotions. The last chapter of the book, "Wisdom and Age," turns to the spiritual part of our being. Memory and memories are what nourish and support the spiritual development of each of us. Without them we would not be able to be in touch with the central core of ourselves, which joins with the body and mind to make up the whole person.

CHAPTER X

Wisdom and Age

"With the ancient is wisdom;
and in length of days understanding."
JOB

Lord, Thou knowest better than I know myself
That I am growing older and will one day be old.
Keep me from the fatal habit of thinking I must
Say something on every occasion.
Release me from craving to straighten out
Everybody's affairs.
Make me thoughtful but not moody; helpful but not
bossy.
With my vast store of wisdom it seems a pity
Not to use it all. . . .
Keep my mind free from the endless recital of details;
Give me wisdom to get to the point.
Seal my lips on my aches and pains. . . .
I dare not ask for improved memory, but a growing
humility. . . .
When my memory seems to clash with the memories
of others,
Teach me the glorious lesson that I may be mistaken. . . .

Give me grace to see good things in unexpected places,
And talents in unexpected people.
And give me, Lord, the grace to tell them so.[20]

"Give me grace to see good
things in unexpected places, and
talents in unexpected people."

This prayer lays out a plan of wise behavior and also reminds us of some of the foibles that can overtake people in their later years. Just because people are old doesn't guarantee that they are wise. Age does not automatically produce wisdom.

"To everything there is a season,
and a time to every purpose
under heaven: A time to be born
and a time to die; A time to
plant and a time to pluck
up that which is planted."
ECCLESIASTES

WISDOM AND SPIRIT—WEAVING
THE STRANDS OF ONE'S LIFE

However, wisdom often does come with age as people remember and make use of their many experiences. They can look back on their lives and see the ways in which they have learned and grown in understanding of themselves and the world they live in. Their wisdom may not come from books, and does not necessarily depend on the amount of schooling they have had. It is the accumulation of living experience, of learning and remembering through success and mistakes. It comes from dealing with the countless responsibilities and changes that a life demands, and from taking advantage of the opportunities to grow that are offered.

The wisdom of long and varied experience sets older people apart from the young—in mature judgment, competence, understanding and acceptance of one's self and others.

"Knowledge comes, but wisdom lingers."
TENNYSON, LOCKSLEY HALL

Older people show their wisdom in many ways, but in the end these ways all seem to depend both on having learned through life experience and on being open to new and future learning. Wisdom develops from the attitudes people have to life, and is expressed in how they live their lives.

In response to the question, "Do you know a wise older person?" someone described his elderly neighbor as a man with inner knowledge rather than book learning. He had a feeling for and an understanding of the seasons, knowing the difference between what is permanent and what changes. He was giving to others but did not give himself away. He was very much his own person, knowing himself and his values.

When a group of seniors were asked to comment on their own wisdom, they had this to say:

—"Wisdom is something I see more easily in others than I do in myself."

—"Wisdom is in how I behave—not only in what I
believe and say but in what I do."
—"Wisdom is helping others without giving advice—
being understanding and not spouting truisms."
—"Wisdom is giving up the lust to be right."
—"I'm wise about some things, not about others.
I'm wise maybe for just a split second."
—"My physical and emotional state determines
whether or not I feel wise on any one day."

SELF-ACCEPTANCE

Old age provides the golden opportunity to finish
weaving the strands of one's life into a whole, com-
pleted pattern. Psychologists who study the spiritual
aspect of aging state the main task of older people is to
take stock of their lives and to come to terms with
them. The inner spiritual wisdom of age comes from
acknowledging the long journey taken. This includes
putting in perspective what is difficult and negative,
as well as the positive things which give satisfaction
and joy. Some things we prefer to forget because they
are painful. Yet if they can be integrated into the
totality of our lives, we begin to see our life's meaning
more clearly. Memory plays the key role in this process.

The person who has integrated his or her life is the
one "who can compromise; who faces small deaths of
life; who finds alternatives when familiar ways become
outmoded; who struggles to grow up throughout life,
facing each life task in each life stage, who continues
to search, always curious, excited to grow and change."[21]

Older people who reminisce about the past are not
just idly rambling. They are often working to bring
together the experiences of a lifetime into a meaning-

ful whole. As people become more aware of their own mortality they pause and look back. Reminiscing helps to integrate the many parts that make up the "me" inside—the child, student, spouse, parent, friend, worker, volunteer, hobbyist, activist, citizen. While reminiscing, people can find themselves asking, "Was it worth it all?" "Did I matter?" "Will people notice or care when I'm gone?" "Did I live a good life?" "If I had to do it again, would I do it in just the same way?" These important questions can be answered only by actively remembering and reviewing the course of one's life.

Memory allows each of us to recognize and value the core of our individuality, our special uniqueness. It helps each of us to be able to say, "I am me and have developed into who I am because of the sum of my experiences." By providing a sense of continuity with our past, memory connects us to our present and gives significance to our future.

The wisdom that comes from this stocktaking and integration often results in an inner serenity and calmness. It deepens our sense of compassion and humility. And it allows us to see the humor in the many absurdities of life. Memory is central to the core of wisdom.

✦

FOOTNOTES

1. Michael J. H. Howe, *Introduction to Human Memory, a Psychological Approach*, p. 94.
2. Bruno Furst, *Stop Forgetting*, 20–21.
3. Brendan Byrne, *Three Weeks to a Better Memory*, p. 93.
4. Laird Cermak, *Human Memory, Research and Theory*, p. 144.
5. Kenneth L. Higbee, *Your Memory, How It Works and How to Improve It*, p. 17.
6. Elizabeth Loftus, *Memory*, p. 15.
7. Mark Brown, *Memory Matters*, p. 47.
8. The Canadian psychologist, Endel Tulving, developed the theory of General Knowledge and Personal Experience Memory under the terms of Semantic and Episodic Memory. Other psychologists have done further research on this theory.
9. adapted from James T. Reason and Klara Mycielska, *Absent-Minded? The Psychology of Mental Lapses and Everyday Errors*, p. 64.
10. Loftus, p. 40.
11. D. W. K. Kay, "Epidemiological Aspects of Organic Brain Disease in the Aged," in Gaitz, Charles (Ed.), *Aging and the Brain*, 15–27.
12. These percentages are estimated, based on readings from Eisdorfer, Gaitz and Storandt.
13. Carl Eisdorfer and Robert O. Friedel (Eds.), *Cognitive and Emotional Disturbances in the Elderly: Clinical Issues*, 81–87.
14. adapted from Joan Mininger, *Total Recall—How to Boost Your Memory*, p. 126.
15. Harry Lorayne and Jerry Lucas, *The Memory Book*, 73–87.
16. Linda Clark, *Help Yourself to Health*, p. 79.
17. Social Planning and Review Council of British Columbia, *Alcoholism and Aging*, p. 2.
18. *Prevention*, January, 1985, 139–40.

19. Loftus, p. 92.
20. A handwritten copy of this poem was offered to us by a member of the senior center where Kathy teaches. According to the donor, it had been recently found after having been tucked away for many years. Most of the poem has been quoted, and we are indebted to its author, whose name we could not track down.
21. Naomi Feil, *Validation—The Feil Method*, p. 18.

SELECTIVE BIBLIOGRAPHY

Popular Books on Memory and Memory Training

Baddely, Alan. *Your Memory—A User's Guide*. New York; Macmillan Publishing Co., 1982.

Brown, Mark. *Memory Matters*. London; David and Charles Newton Abbot, 1977.

Byrne, Brendan. *Three Weeks to a Better Memory*. Philadelphia; The John Winston Co., 1951.

Furst, Bruno. *Stop Forgetting*. Garden City; Doubleday and Co., 1979.

Garfunkel, Florence, and Gertrude Landau. *A Memory Retention Course for the Aged—Guide for Leaders*. Washington, D.C.; National Council on Aging, 1981.

Higbee, Kenneth L. *Your Memory, How It Works and How to Improve It*. Englewood Cliffs, N.J.; Prentice-Hall, 1977.

Loftus, Elizabeth. *Memory*. Reading, Mass.; Addison-Wesley Publishing Co., 1980.

Lorayne, Harry, and Jerry Lucas. *The Memory Book*. New York; Stein & Day Publishers, 1974.

Minninger, Joan. *Total Recall—How to Boost Your Memory*. Emmaus, Pa.; Rodale Press, 1984.

University of Michigan Hospitals, Turner Geriatric Clinic. *Facts and Fiction About Memory*. Ann Arbor, Michigan; 1983.

Books of Related Interest

Alzheimer's Disease—A Family Information Manual. Health & Welfare Canada, Mental Health Division, Health Services Directorate in cooperation with the Société Alzheimer Society.

Clark, Linda A. *Help Yourself to Health*. New York; Pyramid Books, 1976.

Feil, Naomi. *Validation—The Feil Method*. Cleveland, Ohio; Edward Feil Productions, 1982.

Ford, Norman. *Lifestyle for Longevity*. Gloucester, Mass.; Para Research Inc., 1984.

McLeish, John A. B. *The Ulyssean Adult—Creativity in the Middle and Later Years.* Toronto; McGraw-Hill Tlyerson Ltd., 1976.

Social Planning and Review Council of British Columbia. *Alcoholism and Aging.* Vancouver, B.C.; 1979.

Theoretical Books

Botwinick, Jack, and Martha Storandt. *Memory, Related Functions and Age.* Springfield, Ill.; Charles C. Thomas Publisher, 1974.

Cermack, Laird S. *Human Memory Research and Theory.* New York; The Ronald Press Co., 1972.

Eisdorfer, Carl, and Robert O. Friedel (Eds.). *Cognitive and Emotional Disturbances in the Elderly: Clinical Issues.* Chicago; Year Book Medical Publishing Inc., 1977.

Guneberg, Michael M., P. E. Morris and R. N. Sykes (Eds.). *Practical Aspects of Memory.* London; Academic Press, 1978.

Halacy, D. S., Jr. *Man and Memory.* New York; Harper and Row Publishers, 1970.

Harris, J. E., and P. E. Morris (Eds.). *Everyday Memory Actions and Absent-Mindedness.* New York; Academic Press (Harcourt Brace Jovanovich Publishers), 1984.

Howe, Michael J. H. *Introduction to Human Memory, a Psychological Approach.* New York; Harper and Row Publishers, 1970.

Hunter, Ian M. L. *Memory.* Baltimore, Md.; Penguin Books, 1957.

Kay, D. W. K. "Epidemiological Aspects of Organic Brain Disease in the Aged" in Gaitz, Charles (Ed.). *Aging and the Brain.* New York; Plenum Publishers, 1972.

Klatsky, Roberta L. *Human Memory: Structures and Processes.* San Francisco; W. H. Freeman and Co., 1975.

Poon, Leonard W., James L. Fozard, Laird S. Cermack, David Arenberg, Larry W. Thompson (Eds.). *New Directions in Memory and Aging—Proceedings of the George A. Talland Memorial Conference.* Hillsdale, New Jersey; Lawrence Erlbaum Associates, 1980.

Reason, James T., and Klara Mycielska. *Absent-Minded? The Psychology of Mental Lapses and Everyday Errors.* Englewood Cliffs, New Jersey; Prentice-Hall, 1982.

Storandt, Martha, I. Siegler, M. F. Elias. *The Clinical Psychology of Aging.* New York; Plenum Publishers, 1978.

ABOUT THE AUTHORS

Kathleen Brittain Gose, M.A., M.S.W., works with groups of older adults. She teaches creative writing and leads classes in personal growth and development for older women.

Gloria Hammerman Levi, M.S. with a concentration in gerontology, works as a gerontology consultant in a care facility and as a free-lance instructor conducting workshops and in-service education.